A Bundle of articles and Blogs On Global Affaires, by Singer, Author, Urban Guru & Security Advisor Trinityroy

1/Creative Progressive Politics over Ancient Suppressive politics.

What is shown in 2017 by the Spanish Government in its dealings with the Catalan Referendum is clear proof, that modern-politics has not kept up with the needs of a modern age.

Another fact that springs forth, is that of a lack of leadership from the European Union in these matters.

At **the founding of the Union**, a guiding principle was that of a Union of Peace. The Monetary Union came second in that principle. When it came to the creation of the Union it was reduced to an economic Union. And that's where the Union already demonstrated a lack of vision. Instead of really creating and marketing a United One-Market Union <u>With a 500 million potential customer base, it simply went for open trade-borders and a single currency.</u>

Instead of putting **Music, Entertainment & the Movie Industry** behind the endeavor, it stuck to **the financial-elite**. Instead of selling Europe to its next generations really as a Union, it merely created a web of consumer & trade rules. Rules that governed from above, do not always apply to the actual reality when implemented, and often create civil tensions. Like the overrated bookkeepers & civil-servants they are, they went hard to work in creating a paper trail.

These primary actions should have warned some citizens of the Union, of the Euro-Commission's lack of creative progressive thinking. We know now it did not! Now, these short-minded geopolitical & strategic actions by **The European-Union** and most present politicians around the World are a dead-give-away for the polarizing World we live in today.

The Catalan referendum is a clear & transparent example of where governments go wrong.

The referendum is a tool in any countries political toolbox. It is never binding and mostly only used as a civil statement towards it's National political leaders. This was already clear when the referendum over the European Constitution was rejected by the citizens of France, Ireland and the Netherlands, and still the constitution was signed into law.

Therefore, **Spain** could have just let the voting take place without any actual direct political consequences?! Even the European Union could have played a part together with the **Spanish Government**, by for instance granting the Catalonian people some steady progressive autonomy within Spain & the Union?!

The subsequent **Police actions** in this matter, are clearly a lack of vision and could erode the Union further or even create terrorist counter actions. Thereby again creating a **cycle of violence** and hardening standpoints between governments and their citizens. This would than only result in a even larger suppressive police apparatus to be paid by these same citizens? *So,...where are the Politicians with solutions?*

The rise and return of 12th Century Nationalism in many Countries around the World, should be seen as proof of faltering Democratic Politics. The Neoliberal & Capitalistic models have not generated a trickle-down-effect and inequality is on the rise. The middle classes are steadily being erased, in order to create a system based on ruling-classes & working-classes. Not a very creative concept at all! It seems our politicians can't seem to get away from simple black-and-white models for our collective societies. While the Business models are being changed faster than those of our societies, the people are caught in the middle between all these arrogant overpaid quibbling parties. The civil tensions are coming from the top-down and create rising polarization between all kinds of groups.

Democratically elected parties are with a democratic system in order to find middle-ground and practical solutions in order to better our daily quality-of-life. At present they are being directed & corrupted into dominating child-play games that serve no long-term purpose and offer no solutions. These ancient minds need to either get with it, or surrender their positions. In a <u>Globalizing World,</u> we all need to close-in on the idea of being **Global-Citizens.** We need to ,'**Act-Local-&-Think-Global**! In light of that sentiment the actions by the Spanish Government & the lack of action by the European Union has no place in Modern-Politics.

2/The lack of EU Leadership creates new criminal structures.

The wave of refugees that has come into the European Union as of late is creating some serious side effects. Especially where it is dealing with the Economic Refugees from Northern African countries like Morocco.

These refugees are not being dealt with in a consequent manner. They are mostly Young-man that originally are just looking for work and a better future. However; because they are left by our governments in a situation where they have no status nor the prospect of a better future here, they are left in limbo and open to abuse and growing frustration.

They are at present being used by so called naturalized nephews and/or relatives in illegal labor schemes as well as put to work as thieves and drugs-dealers. These European family members are also creating well hidden tent-camps all over Europe in parks and along train-tracks to ,'house', their new army of criminals. Furthermore the Police cannot prosecute these young-man because of their lack off status.

These youngsters went through maddening bureaucratic systems without getting any perspective on a better future. This will frustrate these young man and because of their age and raging hormones they are also becoming perceptive to radical imams and their extremist views.

At present there are many thousands of these youngsters drifting all over Europe, because we did not catch them at the points of entry. The Politicians are leaving the citizens & local Police within the Union, to deal with these growing tensions.

This also creates a problem for actual war-refugees. These real refugees are now being regarded through the same glasses by the Unions citizens as the Economic-refugees.

However it needs to be noted that almost all terror attacks in Europe have been perpetrated by radicalized economic refugees and not the actual war-refugees.

So where are the return boats for these refugees?

They are becoming a bigger and more explosive problem to the entire Union, and are becoming more organized as time goes by.

We need direct action and real leadership to resolve these issues before they disrupt our Nations any further and push Europe into a totalitarian system & a perpetual state of emergency. This will not serve our already eroding democratic system or the future of our common security within the Union.

A concerned citizen of the European Union.

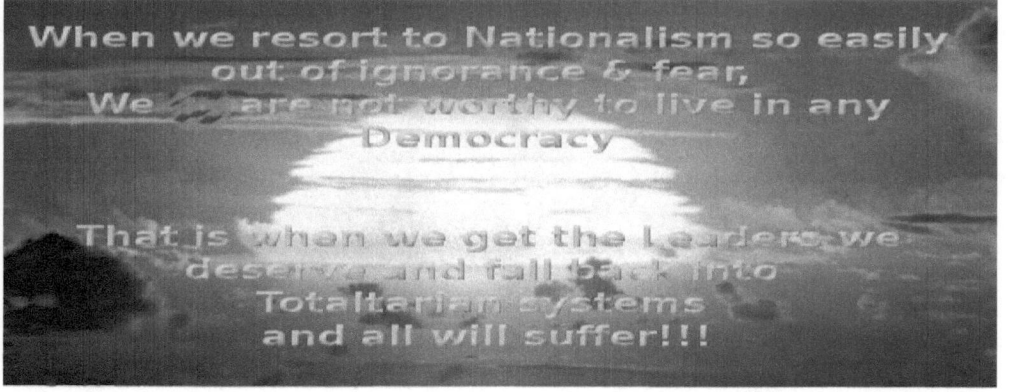

When we resort to Nationalism so easily out of ignorance & fear,
We are not worthy to live in any Democracy

That is when we get the Leaders we deserve and fall back into Totalitarian systems and all will suffer!!!

The Lord must be so disappointed, I know I am.

The way we People are letting ourselves be played against one another is retarded. As a species we hardly seem to become smarter. Socially more awkward yes. By putting our faiths into the hands of computers and gadgets before we use our own minds, will undoubtedly put us on a sliding scale into oblivion. Are we really letting ourselves to be forced into perpetual conflict for the pleasure of the Elite1%. Only so that they can say; See we were right these monkeys deserve to die. They can't even find ways to live in harmony within their own communities. They are and always have been tribal retards.

You and your silly ignorant group-behaviour. The group behaviour that throughout our collective history has been used by tyrants & dictators to play us against one another. The same group behaviour that was used to burn presumed witches is the same hysterical group behaviour we still see when we watch the behaviour of hooligans, nationalists or religious fanatics. Mostly young man & woman driven by a lack of control of their own hormonal glandular systems. Young man & woman that lack a sense of responsibility towards themselves, others or the World around them. And the modern day parents do not seem to be able to cope with the speed of overall developments. Failing to also properly raise their children. Failing to install the right set off values & morals. And while failing individually, we now are seemingly failing as a collective. Our modern societies are falling apart at the seams. The social cohesion is eroding at an ever faster pass.

Instead of coming together as Humans, we let ourselves be divided into sub-minorities, thereby allowing the powers that are, to divide us all even more and rendering us powerless. Instead of collectively fighting for human-rights we now fight for gay, black, woman, or religious rights. Machiavelli would be proud of our collective ignorance. We obviously do not deserve a future for all!

We Need to leave our colonial mentality behind us once and for all. We need to undergo some evolution from Tribal Monkey, Neanderthal, Homo Sapiens, into a Universal Citizen!

4/ ,'We The People',

We The People means nothing when we stay divided. It has no meaning if we do not fight for all our collective rights. Brotherhood, Equality & Liberty for All! If not that than surely the pits of hell for us all.

We will destroy our home planet and nothing will survive to venture into the Universe. Nothing except for a few micro bacteria, maybe.

At present we are rapidly descending into chaos. We need to slow down Global processes of Industry and Capitalism. We really need to stop the arms-race.

The global arms-trade is speeding us all towards a certain collapse of all societies. The arms-trade is closely connected to drugs-trade, corruption, slavery & human-trafficking. We need to stop making, spreading & watching these macho-retarded movies as made in the US. Send all those aggressive & useless images back to their makers. They are not macho or strong, but just the proof of their cowardly fear. They have to hide behind their weapons & movies like a child hides behind it's mothers skirts. Their movies are without function or purpose towards our societies. They produce & promote ignorance, violence, corruption, slavery and overall frustration. They are not educational in any way. We need to start feeding our children some healthy brain-food & real education again.

No more false heroes that shoot up entire cities in these movies, with no regards to the world around them. No more empty dreams and empty outcomes. They are marketing lies without any purpose, but to make money for ruthless investment-bankers & shareholders. It is beyond dirty. It is beyond disgusting. It is beyond any humanity. It is the devil incarnate.

Many of our present business-models are working on the sustained suffering of others. What would happen if cancer was cured? Or if there was no more war? Or, if we would cure most diseases? What jobs would be left? Or would we refocus our efforts on just creating, rebuilding and harmonizing our societies? We would still need doctors, construction workers, technicians, bakers, farmers and such! Let's refocus our efforts away from the narrow-minded tribal & gangster thinking that is leading us now. For God sake stop putting economics before people. It has resulted in childish constant economic tug-of-wars between neighbouring Nations. It is undermining any believe in a future healthy civilization. It makes people become fatalistic.

The opposite outcome when we do nothing could be; People slaughtering one another without any empathy left, while the elite1% hides behind fences until it's all over and feasts on the filthy remains of the rotting corps called Earth. So stop feeding these doomsday narratives to one another and see the real possibilities for all. A cleaner and more harmonious Global society where all can prosper.

Don't worry about population growth, science has already proven the numbers will go down before the end of this century.

Create new goals on the horizon and lay to waist the macho narrow-minded thoughts of the past. You are One People. With different States Of Minds, yes. But still of the same species. So stop buying into doomsday scenarios and stop fighting one another. There will always be natural disasters on this living planet. Let's stop making Life harder by also fighting each-other.

Restore real faith and give hope, because

it has always been easier to destroy than to create.

The snifilized society
Is not civilized.

Mandatory drug tests for all politicians, Now!

5/ <u>Algorithms Marketing & Mind Manipulation.</u>

<u>Polarizing Effects Of Search Engines</u>

....

To get straight to the point; we people are not so great in interpreting our emotions and Chemical unbalances into conversations. Communication is mostly still an infantile exchange of mostly badly chosen words.

As such we are still largely caught-up in wars. Religious, Economic or Territorial conflicts. The Industrialization & digitization of our societies has confronted our juvenile communication skills, with the addition of even more confusing algorithms.

These algorithms as designed by us in order to facilitate revenue & sales, are constructed in such a manner that they are feeding individuals with information and data that the algorithm perceives as important to the consumer and therefor the marketing purposes of products, preferences in politics or otherwise. The fact that this ,'from recent revelations', polarizes people, elections, politics and entire societies is hardly being recognized.It seems to narrow our individual perspectives, rather than widen them.

<u>Social Media</u> makes us seemingly communicate less profound and allows for quick superficial emotional unfounded & uneducated interactions. Recent Elections in Europe and the US have clearly shown, growing tunnel-vision on all sides. <u>A recent Facebook study demonstrates that the polarization phenomenon also applies to this social network</u>.

It seems that the younger generations are actually even displaying more radical points-of-view than their many of their parents before them.

This research does not even include the use of Trolls by opponents of one or another conviction. That are just adding salt in open wounds. All of these factors are driving humanity apart and depicting shallow doomsday scenario's wherein all what we actually seem to do, is should louder and think less.

What we would need is some Normalization or Detente.

So will we just keep going forward into a growing uncertain World or take a step back and review our present collective direction of choice?!

We can obviously not continue creating ever more narcissistic psychopath neoliberal ego's. This will and is affecting the fabric of our respective societies and the Global Human Evolution in it's entirety.

The News media does not properly understand the effects of their constantly repeating news items on both TV & the Net either. The repetitive nature of modern corporate news media, creates more problems than it does solve. Media feeds us the taste of sensation of any certain day into easy to digest one-liners. Hardly ever do they take the time to properly inform us on any issue. Educating us on all sides of matters as well as journalism should be doing, anymore!

All In all we are in dire need of some reviews on our use of and implementations of Social Media & Algorithms as well as News Media and it's impact on modern society.

Rather sooner than later!

The arrogance of us people displays it's ugly head every century.

In this the 21ˢᵗ century our past mistakes and overestimation's might really do us in.

This might be the case for example in the application of antibiotics. Antibiotics were once hailed as the miracle medicine that would protect mankind from all Global outbreaks. **Much like the blind faith we have shown in vaccines, now** superbugs come forth out of antibiotics

We are creating Antibiotic-resistant Superbugs **Research by for example the German** ARD ,'Die Story im Ersten', environmental pollution by Big Pharma is creating a time-bomb worse than any war we ever witnessed. Production spill in China & India are flowing straight into rivers and oceans.

We never considered that we were fighting bacteria where some had actually formed a symbiotic relationship **with us. Let me** take the flu as an example; **The Flu is a nuisance. However it also helps our bodies prepare for the changing of the seasons. Our lungs and respiratory system on the changing temperatures and humidity in the air we breath. Maybe we had already developed a symbiotic relationship with this virus over the many centuries mankind & the virus inhabited the same space. At a certain point we turned this friend into an enemy by attacking it with antibiotics. The virus pushed back and adapted and mutated to attack back, by becoming one of mankind's bigger possible future threats. Proving again we people are not as clever as we think. This hypothesis does not even consider the tinkering we are doing, in badly guarded science labs with these same viruses.**

We always seem to run before we even are able to walk!

The same can be said about the way we started growing our food after the introduction of the industrial revolution, by implementing the use of enormous easy to harvest <u>mono-cultures.</u>

When we took out the <u>plant-life diversity</u> in growing, we made the plants more susceptible to attacks by diseases and insects. Sure we could grow bigger, faster and harvest easier than before. And we did make some people get rich quickly. What again we did not do, is think of the possible long-term effects on soil depletion, fungal attacks or pest crop resistance.

<u>We need to return to Biodiversity in Agriculture and an overall more local approach.</u> The Future Of Food-Security will be in local small farms as well as in Vertical & Urban Farming!

As usual we just dive in at the deep-end and run with it. The same way we did with, nuclear energy, fossil fuels, plastics, asbestos, pesticides, GMO's, etc, etc. Obviously we mostly live in the now, and NO we do not care enough about the future of our children.

<u>The answer</u> would be to listen closer to our senses in looking for healthy long-term solutions, instead of running with every single new invention like it's a Godsend. We are so focused on short-term profits & economy that we lose sight of long-term well being. We could potentially destroy our collective future. Personally I believe *smaller farms , urban-farming & local growing is the solution to Global food-security* issues. I also believe that some flu outbreaks should kill some older people as intended by mother nature. Rooting out the weak, thereby giving way for the next generations. *As long as we keep on putting profits before common sense we can forget about a more harmonious collective future.*

<u>So I think the more general question is;</u> are we actually becoming smarter or are we becoming a degraded result of our actual potential? Are we really making progress, or are we merely talking one another into believing we are? Are we lacking the courage to take responsibility for our individual and collective actions, leaving this up to insurance companies, the judicial-system & multinationals? We need to think before we ink! We need to educate and develop into single growing individuals as part of a collective that shows real progress into a combined and healthy future wherein we can all benefit of our many individual inventions and solutions.

The only way to do so, is to put people before economic targets and stop Nationalistic tug-of-wars between sovereign Nations. <u>Capitalism has failed human-rights, the environment and progress in general.</u> If anything capitalism has hampered mankind and slowed-down progressive action on many matters concerning us all. Dualism & competition should only serve enhancements not create some winners and countless losers. So take a good look at our actions before we start running in order to have the time to first visualize possible errors in our thinking. Stop kissing ass and create space for constructive criticism. This is the way forward to healthy answers and a more healthy future for all.

Gadgets being used as extensions of our senses should not inhibit the expansion or growing awareness of these same senses.

Think Global,...... Act Local!   It is not an empty philosophy!

6/ We The People,… are we worthy of Democracy?

All over the Planet Authoritarian rule is on the rise.

What is the reason for this retreat into protectionism and nationalism? Why, has the system of Democracy lost it's appeal? Is it not the best system we have at present for basic human dignity and civil rights? Why would people freely choose to step back into the dark ages of fascism & nationalism? There are many underlying causes we can pin-point, however the most obvious one is the polarizing force of failed trickle-down-economics and capitalism. They have divided people by increasing inequality, false austerity programs and self-induced economic crisis.

We-The-People are failing, each other.

We let ourselves be lured into empty and unfounded dividing discussions on social media. All so eager to ventilate our frustrations, we actually play into the cards of the financial-elite and start fighting one-another?! Over the most silly subjects and issues we foul-mouth and stimulate the divide. Obviously we have learned nothing from history. **This is ancient Roman and Machiavellian knowledge. Rule by divide still works after hundreds of years.**

Why,...? Because you are all too stupid to enjoy the benefits of a healthy Democracy. Democracy needs maintenance and vigilance. It does not stay sound and healthy by itself, it needs the people to come together for a common goal & purpose. This is a Fact!!!

Still you all think in terms of Left or Right wing Democratic parties, or Conservatives against progressive thinkers. This only breeds more radicalism and even extremism. Extremism does not create itself, it is a reaction to growing inequality.

In the meantime your so called chosen representatives do not represent you, but are simply looking for a nice job in the private sector, worn down by all the industry lobbyists that constantly surround them. **Politicians have been selling-out the Environment, Foodsafety and your Health for a few short-term profit-margins and their corporate seats. They are plunging the entire World and Mankind into an ocean of false security and rising tensions and pollution,** only because they do not come together and make the appropriate decisions that need to be made for our common collective futures. Politicians are over-payed and over-valued and lack decisive action. They should stick to bookkeeping and supporting infrastructural works & logistics, leaving daily lives and the rule of law to the judges and justice systems. They definitely should stop meddling so much in everybody's daily lives creating more problems than solving them, dragging us all down into Police-States with their unfounded Panic-Politics. We should make it so that politicians can be held accountable for their mistakes and this goes for CEO's of transnational corporations as well. We need Corporate-accountability as well as Political-accountability. Where are the cases against polluting Multi-Nationals, Chemical Giants and Energy suppliers. **Where is their accountability?**

Where is a real International-Court-Off-Law to punish Crimes-Against-Humanity? If we as a World do not solve these outstanding issues we will drag the entire World into chaos and all will suffer! We-The-People should stop making the same mistakes as the politicians, ventilating and meddling in affairs we do not know nothing about. Educate yourselves first or shut the.. Up!

The levels of frustration have reached unprecedented levels, so you all need to come together on the main issues and move away from an economic tug of war between nations.

Economic-warfare will kill us all and Economic Growth can not go on forever without hurting other Nations & People in the process.

You the people need to make sure that rising technical know-how benefits all in the World and not just a few. If that means revolutions, demonstrations or getting hurt in the process, let it be so! Because what we are doing NOW has an expiration date. We need to move away from this doomsday thinking into systems that create rather than destroy. We have the knowledge and just need to implement it. We can have clean water, food, sanitation and shelter for all within the next fifty years. But only if we move away from the ignorant way we are all behaving at present. At present we are unworthy of a common shared Democratic & positive future. We-The-People is at present an empty phrase at best. It is and has been used for centuries to move us apart and unless we find ways to learn from our past mistakes and find common ground, we will plunge this our home planet into oblivion.

So the choices are clear: to all you junkies and slaves of the system caught-up in games of meaningless fear and intimidation.

WiseUp!

Show to your children that you are the grown-ups you pretend to be!

Stop to overestimate your individual intelligence and combine the knowledge of ages into working-models that can benefit our entire species. It Can Be Done!

We had a mean 2016
As Mean as they come & and as mean as I've seen
We Rattled we Rolled too many stories untold.
And as entire countries through austerity were sold,
We saw the greed and hate unfold,
While little man in grey suits pretended to negotiate,
Peace & Humanrights were trampled under the pretence of Faith.
While through arms & drugstrade the tiet of finance flourished,
Love & understanding got severely undernourished.
While so many got influenced by the actions of so few,
the media enlarged & Politicians did not know what to do.
While most are happy to have but basic needs,
the greedy kept on manipulating our seeds.
Still Looking for World domination,
the Elite sealed their own faith and by doing so dragged us all down
into a rat-race using frustration & hate.
And while gadgets & carrots still dangle in front of our eyes,
we fail to see the reason of our own demise.
Although the logic is clear, it gets lost in a message of fear.
And next year,..... what will YOU do?
In 2017 who will you be listening to?
Or will most just sit back and ...... continue,.....? Trinityroy2016

7/ Society and Sociopaths

In every group of people there is always one single sociopath. One person that lacks the ability for empathic behaviour towards others. One human with a glitch, much like a mental illness with narcissistic tendencies.

At present in this the 21st century, the balance has shifted. No longer we have just a few greedy sick fools amongst us, no; our western modern societies have become riddled with way too many problem cases. And what's worse, we now teach this insane mentality to our off-spring. We actually teach the next generations to not give a damn. We do it in macho superficial movies, games & TV-series. We see it especially in the results coming forth from our financial institutions and the way our elected politicians give preference to economics before, people, food-safety or the environment? This way spreading the mental disease into the real World.

Since the start of the Industrial revolution, several new factors came to play in how we developed our societies. One of those factors is the fact that Industrial strategies prefer to work with set boundaries and simple to divine targets. It divides people into target-groups such as religious,sexual preference, skin color, young/old, male or female and such. It simplifies and takes the nuance out of life and living to facilitate it's own business-models. It does this with no consideration to the consumers or customers, placing their own objectives before the needs of the collective and it's future. These protocols as created by Industrial targets actually did dumb down the working of our society towards living as a collective. This becomes evermore apparent over time, when the result are becoming clear for all to see.

Now; together with these factors as mentioned before we have the influence of a totally new factor coming into play: The use of narcotics and particularly cocaine. Cocaine feeds the ego and dumbs-down the senses. As it is mostly laced with speed or amphetamines that tends to create paranoia, it becomes clear to see why so many ambitious people made this their drug of choice. The regular use of this drug also permanently alters the way it's users think and behave towards others in their surroundings.

Over the last 35 to 40 years many in <u>power positions in Politics</u>, Finance, Law and many other professions have given in to the trap of this drug. It is not just a problem of the poor, it has affected the higher regions of governance of our Democracies as well. And that created many of the problems we are facing today. Tests have been run in both the House of Lords in the UK and the <u>buildings of the European Union</u>. These tests were made in the toilets allocated to staff only, and in 60% of them residue of cocaine was found. So it´s use is not just limited to private time, but also takes place during working hours. Probably to deal with the stress of living amongst other sociopaths and their ego´s. These political leaders are in charge of making laws and keeping transnational-corporations at bay. They need to safeguard the citizens against pollution of our food-chain and environment. Against corruption & fraud. They are and have been creating the Economic Wars that have created so much suffering. It has become clear that politics in recent decades has failed Democracies and in the foreseeable future, mankind.

They have become greedy and rather than playing a mediating role have become part of the problem. They played citizens into polarizing minorities, by the old Machiavellian rules of divide and conquer. The only difference is that now everybody plays these retarded games, not just Kings & Conquerors! This now has resulted in the biggest arms-race ever in our human history! The general pollution of our planet, continues Economic Wars and humanity more divided & with more displaced people than ever before. Instead of selling a sane image of Democracy to the World as we did after WorldwarII, we now are Globally depicted as deprived sick societies at war with ourselves, hardly better than communists or dictators. Corporations want to take over the Governance and stand over Governments trough criminal trade-deals. These trade-deals would give even more power to these transnationals and make Governments & People subordinate to their business-models. These are crimes against humanity and our collective future.

The least we could do, is have mental checks of all of those in power as well as regular drug-testing on hard-drugs for all our civil servants. Those in Banking, Pension-funds Insurance and such, need to be kept at bay by strict rules and regulations. At present it seems there are more rules for the average taxpaying citizen than for all these greedy money-hungry sell-outs to their own kind. This is an unbalance that needs to be rectified for Democracy to ever work again. No more non-profit NGOs with insane wages for their CEO's. Insane wages are just a legalized bookkeeping trick for so called non-profit organizations to rob the people blind.

Legalized corruption is one of the biggest problems the World an mankind face at present. Bureaucracy has only created more loopholes for these enterprises to take advantage off. Lobbying needs to be banned from Politics as well, for sanity to return in Democratic systems. Anything else is just another scam.

So in short: *Drug-testing for all civil-servants, *caps on wages for all non-profit CEO's, *Corporate liability to deal with transnational crimes and *restoring secular Democratic values for all, in order to be able to sell Democracy around the World again as the only sane option.

8/ The Minority Polarizing Trap

The word minority has brought the World more divide than Unite!

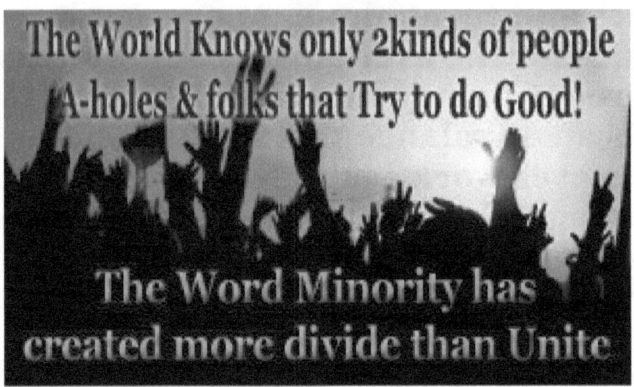

For what is a minority if not part of humanity? It seems to me that we have not been integrating but rather polarizing public opinion over the last few decades. We see it in most depictions coming out of America as seen in movies and on TV with all their stereotypes. All black or all Latino or all white soaps as well as the idea of Gay-Pride-Parades. All of these are more freak-shows than a show of diversity & humanity. The worst effect they produce is a counter-effect by other radical movements or out of plain individual ignorance.

Even in the developing World the emphasizing of minorities has led to lesser integration, not only of gays but also in religious acceptance. Where before religious minorities or gay communities, had been living amongst other religious majorities for centuries, we now see rising tensions between all folks of different creed, color, religion or sexual preference Worldwide. I honestly hope that the US lack of cultural understanding and meddling in the World does not drive us all into another World War.

What we all need now is ,'nuance', in rhetoric and to CELEBRATE DIVERSITY. No more,'One Liners', that serve only to fill time-slots for News-media. No more singled-out this or that pride-parades; ending up mostly in wasteful consumer parties that provoke more than they actually do help to integrate and mostly just paint distorted pictures.

Now we all know that people tend to drift towards tribal group clusters, for various reasons. Mostly out of fear, peer-pressure or a false sense of security. We hide within these groups mostly not because we choose to, but because that is just the ruling local or National mantra. This keeps us from becoming a collective of individual thinkers. This is what keeps us from becoming a collective of Global Citizens.

Industry, Insurance companies and Governments also play into these sentiments. Industry prefers easy to cater-to groups. Easy to facilitate needs & preferences. This clearly segregates us into categories that did not exist before the Industrial Revolution. It makes our daily lives less colourful and does not enrich society as a whole. It is actually closer to a fascist model than a divers society model. This is also clearly taking place through insurance companies. If you are not insured your are no part of society and if you can be insured depends on what group you belong to?!

So in conclusion. I prefer a ,'PEOPLE-PRIDE-PARADE'. soundtrack

I prefer a divers and colourful society to any simplified but rather dull & boring and possibly dangerously categorized humanity, anytime! I will never accept federal fascist models created just to please some industrial elite and their corrupt cronies. These models lack any & all intellect and will never be able to bring humanity into a brighter future that works for us all.

So let's all stop to talk for a moment and let all present created Global tensions come to an ease, a détente. We are all in need of an easing of tensions and the geopolitical arrogance that has been going around. We need real role-models for man-kind. Therefore Again: let's create that PEOPLE-PRIDE-PARADE and show the WORLD the diversity & real wealth of mankind.

Trinityroy info portal

9/ Fire & Water

"Welcome to Planet Earth"

Welcome to a violent Planet full of Life. Fire & Water cannot exist within the same space, yet side by side they are the creators Life. What does that say about us Humans?! Is this also why we are so violent? Or do we just still lack comprehension of our surroundings in general? Yeah, Let's stick with that version.

It's like what I always say; Recognize the Devil inside you, if you want to become able to do good. There is no Saint without a Devil. We cannot hide from our origins. We are born from Water & Fire.

So,.. is that also why we people stay locked in perpetual wars & conflicts? I do not believe that, that is the case. We are just an infantile mostly still ignorant race. By not accepting our opportunistic, envious, greedy side, we seem to get stuck in tribal emotions and mass stupidity. These emotions are easily manipulated by the most evil ones amongst us, for their own shallow goals & purposes. The only tower of babel and cities of Sodom & Gomorrah have been created & sustained by us all, collectively. The lack of control of our individual emotions have been the only reason for us to stay as retarded as we have been. Even our lack of skills in communication is a direct result form us lacking control & awareness of our bodies chemistry & emotions.

And while we as a species need to take the next step in our collective evolution, we constantly get slowed down by our own fellow human beings. We waist time and opportunity on a Global scale. So it's not so crazy to conclude that we are not as smart as we think ourselves to be.

At present there are two scientific pathways being explored in our efforts to live with and in Nature. One is called Geoengineering and the other Geo-Design. The 1st tries to make nature do what we want it to do, and the other tries to design alongside with nature. The 1st so called science is a typical case of human arrogance and God-like thinking while the other,'design', is just trying to better our lives without manipulating entire weather patterns and such.

It is the same as when we cross-breed plants to make them better resistant for certain pests or weather circumstance, or whether we manipulate their genetic DNA strands in order to supposedly make them do what we want. The so called GMO's. And we do not actually know their long-term effects on our environment.

It seems there too many so called ,'Doctor Mengele's', in the World, that only do care about their short-term profits more than what we leave behind for the next generations. The results of this ignorant greed is already affecting our daily lives all around us. We see it in; Plastic, Asbestos, Nuclear and many other chemical pollutants that are now rampant in nature, creating diseases and affecting our common food-chain.

In the meantime the Arms-Industry fuels it's polluting wars & conflicts. These are all reflections of our common inner Devil. A direct result of our collective stupidity. We are quickly losing time and although we do have all the technical know-how to change are course, it seems we lack the courage and will to do so. We are as much Evil as we are Good. It is and always will be up to us to find a working balance. However if we fail to see we are & do, we will never start to develop into something better and become good.

We need to find better ways to communicate and find middle ground. We need to steer away from radicalism & extremism. Stop feeding sensation lusted news agencies, that serve no purpose but their own. Multi-National-corporations that want to forever expand their economic influence at any cost. Career Politicians that do not take responsibility for their actions and the laws they implement on their citizens. We need to see these Devils for what they are and call them out. Some Fires need to be cleansed with Water. We Need to become a Global-Community.

Neither Fire nor Water are all bad. Neither the Devil or Saints are all bad or all good. It is up to us to find the middle ground and come to creation. That is our task and responsibility.

You and your body are both Fire & Water, living in harmony. Now stop acting like fools. And,'Make It So',

10/ Power Corrupts

Every time any individual gets any kind of power he or she loses sanity and becomes corrupted. Personally I have lost all faith in mankind. We have seen it through the ages and in our modern industrialized World, and now corruption has become so much worse than ever before in our collective History.

Most of us grown-ups behaving like infantile children that did not receive enough attention from their parents, when they were young.

Governments and Big Business:

This has become ever more clear within our respective Governments and Political systems. We see how overpaid formerly called ,'**civil-servants**', increasingly are behaving like arrogant little kings and queens. Lacking all common sense and never taking responsibility for their actions or the lack of action; Government officials are a major contributor to growing civil tensions in society. And they spend taxpayers money as if it was their own. They are slowing down real healthy economic projects and making daily live for the average citizen or entrepreneur into a living hell filled with regulation enforced by lower educated officers. Edging us ever closer to a new form of fascism.

The other problem is their lack of knowledge of whatever projects Government officials spent tax-money on. Failing investments and overdrawn budgets have become more the rule than the exception. And their wages & pension-plans did go up, while the average taxpayers has gained nothing or even lost spending power. It 's as crooked and sick as never before. These same **civil servants have also contributed to corporations becoming more corrupt than ever, selling out to corporate lobbyists. Thereby destroying both our environment and civil cohesion.**

We say we want to do good, until we do accumulate some wealth and than do everything in our individual powers, to not lose that, or even increasing that same material wealth. We do not show any interest or care what happens to others as long as we ourselves are able to grow richer.

Politics: The new Political Neo-Liberal mentality is the worst of them all. It does not care about anybody but themselves and takes narcissism to another level. They are similar to Cocaine users. These people have no real friends and can never be trusted. Not to Family, Friends or even themselves. They will do anything to gain wealth or power, even if it means selling their bodies or souls. They are the sharks, rats and hawks of our time. The predators!

They are the flies that feed of the shit and carcasses of others. They have too be cut down to size or eliminated from our society or they will fester like a carcinogen or other major disease. They have no long-term vision and live by the day, only. They are the most professional ass-kissers and sociopathic charmers you will ever encounter. They appear to be nice until you feel their knives in your back or their fists up your arse. They Kiss up, in order to be able to fuck,.. down! They lack real intelligence, but believe themselves to be both smart & great? The worst result from corrupt politicians is growing support for right-wing-radical parties as is happening at present in Europe and America.

We need to *stop worshipping these fraudulent fake-gods* and start to see them for what they are. Misfits and egomaniacs that will not contribute to a positive evolution of our species. They will keep on harming others & the environment around them as long and as hard as they can. If we do not put a stop to these sick souls, they will drag us all down into growing chaos and eventually oblivion.

Look back at History and remember the Napoleon's and Hitlers, that were nothing less than frustrated pathetic little fucks. But these social misfits did drag millions of people with them into massive mortality rates and even more suffering.

Many of these so called ,'World Leaders', were often nothing more than pathetic little drug users. We need to learn from History and stop repeating the same mistakes.

We owe it to ourselves and our children to break the vicious cycle of suffering and destruction we have submitted to for far too long. We have the technical know-how to **create a better future for all**. It is possible and should be done NOW! To wait another century is not an option. There is no over-population. There is no need for wars no more. There are only greedy little bastards that keep us all from evolving into better humans. Actions make the man not a rolex or big car. This is childish frustrated behaviour that serves only a corrupt **consumer based capitalist society not worthy of any future**. It is narrow-minded and without any sound basis to build upon. Take action and buy nothing that is advertised. **Go for real quality of live and not the pimps OG and hooker mentality** that serves only the man and his greed.

Take on the Banks, Governments and Insurance companies for not representing their clients and citizens. Make them pay fort their corrupt role in harming us and the environment for so many decades. They have proven beyond a shadow of a doubt they cannot be trusted. Treat them accordingly. It is time we the People start to play our role in society and no longer their twisted little power & greed games.

This all really is possible, unless it turns out we are already beyond help and have become so mentally masochistic sick, we might as well collectively walk into the furnaces of oblivion and perish.

The choice is still yours, ... we The People need to take responsibility for the future ourselves and not just appoint some leaders in order to avoid that responsibility.

Now make real quality into a reality4All !

11/ Democracy versus Capitalism

Democracy is under it's most heaviest attack since it was perceived. Never before has greed eroded our liberal foundations, as it does in this the 21st Century. It has turned into a true battle between ideologies (If you can call GREED an ideology?). Economic warfare between Nations almost seems the new normal. But it is not! It could bring the entire evolution of us humans to it's knees. It could be our collective downfall.

While most of our fellow humans are still living in poverty and without basic facilities like infrastructures for running water or energy, others are playing with the latest high-tech gadgets, the latest high-tech cars and houses & living in shameless wealth. This with no regard to the suffering of millions of others. The elite is de-humanized, de-sensitized and even considers killing anybody that stands in the way of their wealth, the new normal. They sell this idea under the excuse off ,'Global Overpopulation'. The arrogance and sociopathic behaviour from so few to so many, is at an all-time high.

Even in the western world, people feel powerless against so much violent behaviour. Suppressed as slaves to Banks, Mortgages, corrupt Politicians & the system they live in, most tend to give up and just go along. Even against their better judgement. The results have been clear for all to see; Worldwide pollution, corruption and growing inequality.

The divide between our kind has gone from bad to worse. No longer it touches creed or colour. It has been subdivided into even more so called minorities like; man/woman Rich/poor Gay/Straight Muslim/Christian Shiite/ Sunni Kurdish/ Turkish and whatever group can be played-out against one another. And as far as being ruled by divide is concerned, nothing has changed there since the colonial conquests.

These actions only resulted in People retreating into new tribal communities out of fear, alongside a mountain of growing chronic diseases, that nobody will want to pay for. To recover from this perverted & polluted mantra of modern society will no doubt take another 100 years. In the meantime people will again not be allowed to grow into a Global community as well they should have.

Multi-Nationals are playing a very questionable role in all this; First the major large economic players have held evolution off our species back for over a century. Like for example; the fossil fuel industry that purposely withheld clean energy from finding ground decades earlier. Companies like Nestle trying to buy up all clean drinking water wells Globally, with no regard to the people living around these wells. Or the Chemical giants like Dow & many others that have uninhibited polluted our soil, oceans and all-round environment. Now these same players say they are part of the clean-energy revolution and want to clean up their act?! How much more corruption and downright lies can our species and the planet take before it all perishes?!

We are but an opportunistic species still stuck in colonial behaviour that is no longer of this time. We need to lose this warped and sick mentality rather sooner than later. We do not have to all become equal! We could never all be equal because this would mean we would lose our capacity to adapt to random situations. However we do need to create a more equal evolutionary process in order to survive as a species. We cannot just create a Ruling-class & Working-class system, because this obviously only leads to civil tensions and wars in our respective societies. It Would be better to create an overall Middle-class society with only a few Higher & lower-classes

Politicians need to be able to hold accountable for their actions as well as CEO's from major corporate players. We need to install International courts that pursue transnational corporate en political crimes as soon as possible. It is not small crimes that threaten our World, but these crimes by major producers & politicians that so far have gone mostly unpunished. We need to set examples that large scale corruption does not pay, or all suffer the consequences.

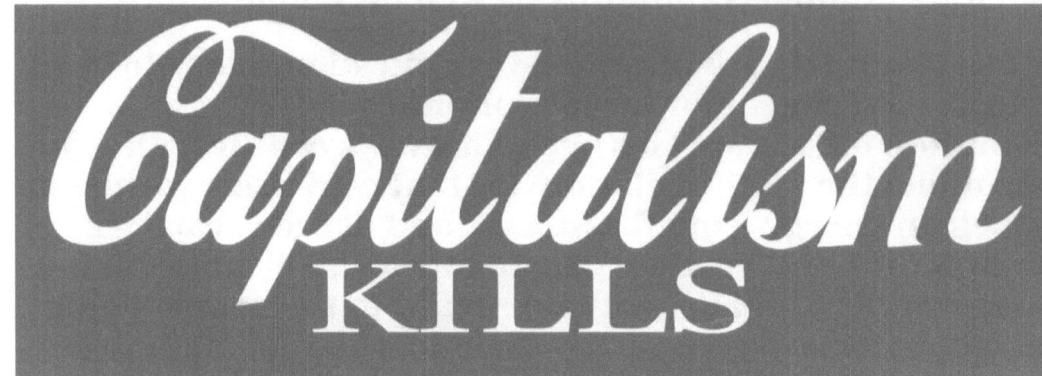

12/Economics Before People, is Killing Humanity

The individual economic tug of war by sovereign Nations has run it's course. It cannot be sustained and is polluting our collective environment as well as causing unspeakable suffering by millions of humans. This is being caused by a culture of greed as well as the paranoia of the western world & especially the Anglo-Saxon countries to lose dominance.

Nations are still thinking in terms of being Empires while Transnational companies are not hampered by any borders at all in doing business. So while the financial- elite is conducting worldwide traffic in business, not even an European Union seems to be able to find unity in political decision making processes.

We have seen what this has meant towards the citizens of this world in environmental damages and the rise of chronic diseases resulting from this. Imagine the costs of these inflicted healthcare issues to our respective societies, if you can. This has also stunned all efforts to integrate people & Nations into a United World.

It has set people against one another turning many into anti-social, a-holes. It is exactly these narrow-minded economic goals that are constantly surpassing the importance of health & welfare that could bring down everything we have accomplished so far and drag us all into another World-war.

Look at the The Fossil-fuel industry that purposely has been keeping the development of clean & free-energy back for at least one-hundred years, thereby throwing the future of our children into uncertainty for hundreds of years to come. These are nothing if not crimes against humanity. These super ,'filthy', rich will probably never be prosecuted for these crimes-against-humanity. But they should be!

We have allowed Politicians to side with Economy and Industry & not Humanity for far too long. Thereby polluting our complete collective ecosystem with, asbestos, plastics, pesticides, nuclear radiation and immense quantities of chemical waste that cannot even be filtered-out of our drinking water any-more. Nice job gentleman! Your grey suits and high-school education did not prevent you from having a short-term vision and lack of imagination.

Look for example at the production processes of luxury goods & gadgets; We produce these in such a manner that they pollute the environment from beginning to end. They will need to be replaced within 5 years to a decade, if not sooner. This of-course also creates much more toxic waste than ever before. Why not make luxury goods that last 50 years or more? Why, because that would slow down economic growth. This is how these short-sighted companies think. This also is why for example, in China now lie 16 of the most polluted cities in the World. Now, how smart is that?

13/ The Stupidity of Typecasting & Stereotypes

People are not simply all Black or All White?! Simply All Straight or All Gay. Live don't work that way. Within being Straight or Gay there are countless differences. It's as if you would say that we know only one kind of tomato or one kind of cabbage, and we know that ain't true! The simplicity of America, Hollywood, News-Media & TV in general and how they have been depicting human individuals is simply retarded and has in no way whatsoever contributed in humanity coming together as one. The 21st Century Western TV has been driving people apart through narrow minded narratives and scriptwriting that lacks logic. All black or all white soap series. A single Arab or one Gay or Colored in TV/shows as silly attempts to seemingly showing you want to bridge gaps?!

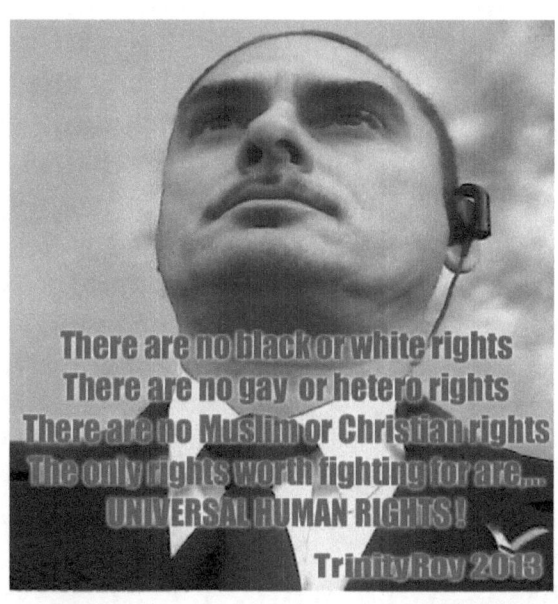

There are no black or white rights
There are no gay or hetero rights
There are no Muslim or Christian rights
The only rights worth fighting for are...
UNIVERSAL HUMAN RIGHTS!

TrinityRoy 2015

By dividing into human subgroups or so called minorities, we have been catering our lifestyles to facilitate the Industry and not people. It has eased the way business could be directed towards certain groups, while at the same time giving way to extremist or radical individuals to more easily target their ignorance towards these minorities. This entire approach to our multicultural species and planet, did not bring us together but drove us further apart than we ever have been before.

It made WE THE PEOPLE into an empty slogan

For example; At one time, I proposed to the city of Amsterdam to replace the Gay-Pride-Parade to be replaced by a People-Pride-Parade. I was immediately met with outrage by those who where making money from the Gay-Pride. I responded with the question, whether what they were doing was to achieve equal rights or a separate status in society? The bottom-line answer was financial gain and had nothing to do with the integration of anything at all. I told the Gay-Pride organizers that their concept as it came over from California USA, did not do me proud as a citizen of Amsterdam & Europe.

I believed than as I do now that we had to create a Floating boat parade that consisted out of the many different cultures that our City has to offer and that this should merely include several boats with Gay & LGBT participants. I also told them that I believe that the present approach has to much of a sexual connotation and is more like a freak-show for provincials to come and watch than it is for-filling it's purpose of integrating Gay people into our general communities. Whatever I said was all to no avail. Preoccupied as they were with short-term profits and not a long-term vision.

This has been the problem with any and all approaches by mass media in general. It creates opposites not mutual individual respect. It enlarges our differences into freakish caricatures.

On local levels worldwide, TV and Media have contributed in driving people apart.

Not just in gender or creed, but also in Religions. Many religions & cultures in the Asian part of our world had been living together in their major cities, until ,'for an example', the televised Arab-Spring highlighted their differences and drove them apart. It set them against one another and lead by a minority of loud mouth radicals, they started cleansing neighbourhoods and entire cities with baseless rage. Frustrations that had their origins in a lack of education, quality of life and failed politics, were transformed into racist & nationalistic rage and polarization. Mass Media and so called news, plays a dirty role in all this. People were and are played against one another, while Politicians & Multinational corporations & financial institutions profit from their suffering selling arms in a growing but ,'false', security industry. With the growing arms & security industry the problems only got worse and turned into a western society that is now based it's economies on the frustrations and sufferings of their citizens.

We are moving away from a well needed growing awareness of being One species on One Planet.

Egomaniacs and sociopaths are our political & business leaders.
(I call upon mandatory drugs-tests for elected government officials)
Caught-up in battles of economics and proxy-wars we move away
from a cleaner environment or finding harmony in our common
existence. We talk the talk, but do never not ,'walk the walk'. The
louder some narrow-minded haters shout, the bigger the airtime they
get on media. History did not teach us anything, it seems. Looking
for cheap thrills and relying ever more on gadgets and not our
senses, we seem to voluntary have thrown the future of our species
onto a slippery slope. To afraid to stop or turn back, we now hurdle
forward into a future ever growing more uncertain.

We need to clean up our acts and see the beauty of our diversity. We people come in many sorts and varieties, with even more individual nuances. It does not matter who you are, or how you feel. What matters is, how you function within your communities, both local & Global.

The only healthy tribe, is a tribe of individuals that are able to think
for themselves and are willing to take responsibility for their
individual actions. No longer we should hide shared responsibilities
behind presidents, kings & queens or even insurance companies that
are supposed to be non-profit. These are all false senses of security
and the will turn around to bite us in our collective asses. Time itself
is the only true judge of our actions. This is already clear to see in
how we polluted our environment and are now dealing with rising
numbers of chronic illnesses. Or our rampant use of antibiotics and
how bacteria and viruses have adapted to them.

We need to grow-up and stop our childish infantile actions
and often baseless emotional behaviour. The way you choose
to live, does not need to be carried out onto the street in front
of everybody to see. This is private and does not need to be on
TV. Mutual respect is generated by dignity not any, in your
face mentality!

Show some sophistication and stop to laugh about others suffering. It only shows your lack of education. Stop provoking and start living together, it is not so hard to do. We need to provide every single person on this planet wit a roof over their heads, running water & sanitation and some food-security before we sell smart-phones and gadgets to the entire world. Get your priorities in order. Infrastructure for all needs to be preferred before countries individual tug-of-war in yearly economic growth. Live is not about Woman-rights, Gender-rights, Black, Asian or Religious rights. Life is about Universal Human-rights in general. All other roads lead to polarization and our common mutual destruction.

BECOME ONE!

UBUNTU!

14/ The lack of culture in the Music Industry

Is this really the best we have to offer our children? This Anglo-Saxon pimped-up domination of the Music-industry?

Hookers, Gangsters, Pimps and thieves? Culturally Impoverished high-end production values depicting Disney girls dressed up as prostitutes? No wonder people in general lose track of what is right in life?! TV & MTV feeds them mental garbage. If you want to create a generation of derailed mentally sick teenagers you only feed them this, as what we are doing at present.

What is the most frustrating in this entire episode of music creation, is how these masters of chaos control the distribution networks. It is close to impossible for anything descent to rise in any music charts anywhere. Even the play-lists for radio stations are completely under the control of major distributing companies. No radio DJ is allowed to play what he actually just found or heard somewhere. Especially in the western hemisphere this is the case.

For example:

In the nineties I as the author of this article wrote to the European Union with the following request; I asked the members of the EU to help me create a European version of MTV. I intended to bring music from the major

European cities in order to create a cultural exchange and enrichment of music productions in general. I wanted to create a platform for up and coming artists and bands from Spain, Germany, France, Scandinavia, Italy, Greece and Serbia and such. This would according to my writing to the Union enhance the exchange of cultures and benefit the Unification of Europe in general.

To my amazement the answer I received from a Miss Vivian Reading's office was short and clear. The European Union does not intend to stimulate, participate, finance or in from or manner contribute to the creation of a European music video channel. I was dumbfounded! They made sure that no healthy competition to the present domination in music creation & distribution could ever take place. What was their interest in that?

What surprised me even more in this answer was the total lack of vision in the role it could have played in a general sense of Unification with the citizens of Europe?! It made me conclude that the European Union was entirely created as a monetary Union and had no intention at all, to create a sense of mutual respect and cultural exchange. So much for the European Union Let alone any integration of music from the East or Asia!

In the meantime the music industry is doing everything to hold on to their dominant position in music creation and distribution. This goes especially for music on radio & TV and music in advertisement. They rule the airwaves and therefore the way to the ears of our children. And although we have made great advancements in production methods, the content is completely lacking any creativity. So what we are listening to and watching is High definition sociopathic anti-social superficial nonsense. It works like training monkeys with flashing lights in many colours while actually not showing anything special at all.

It is mostly mentally sickening and socially worthless garbage. It will not stand the test of time.

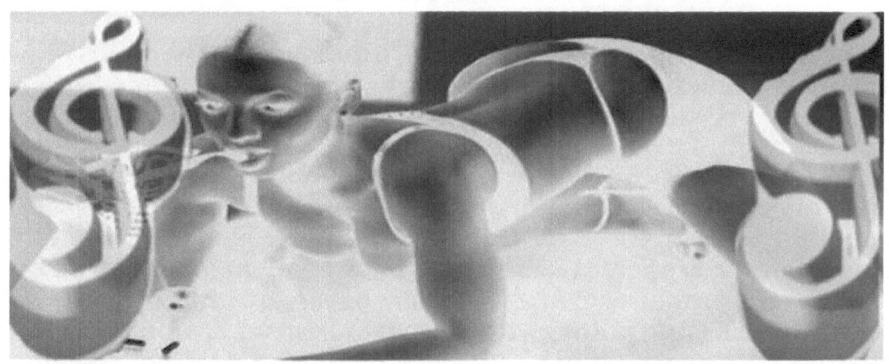

So again I ask you the reader and the many broadcasting stations world-wide: Is this really what you want to leave to the next generations as your 21st century legacy? Is this the best you can do, or are you also in the creation of music waiting to be bested by the Asian countries? Any Bollywood movie-star already has 10 times more fans than any Hollywood actor. Did you know that? And what about the African continent? Do you really belief you can conquer that long-term with your silly US UK artists?

These 21st century music products are not timeless like those created in the sixties & seventies. And most important of all, they lack culture. They do nothing for example for womans-rights or education. They are completely critic-less of changes in our modern societies and utterly shallow. So; for all the quality production methods developed by our industry, our music got left behind stuck in a swamp of politicized Geopolitics promoting nothing but frustration and consummation. What a sad result for such a promising start.

I honestly hope we can break this Anglo-Saxon domination of the music market and create some better role-models and better music for our future generations.

15/ Meltingpot Europe

The Union & the Refugee Crisis

There is nothing wrong with the multicultural society. There never was. It is the lack of leadership by politicians that creates friction within our societies. They are solely to blame for the rise of Nationalism, radicalism and fearmongering.

The present refugee crisis in Europe is a prime example of Brussels lack of leadership. When the exodus from the middle-east started and the influx began, the European Union could have implemented raised border controls and proper registration too separate economic from war refugees at the crossing points within weeks. Instead it took them months and still now they are dealing badly with the given situation. Hereby they give way to finger-pointing and rising social tensions.

The Western News media does it's part here as well and provides a platform to the biggest, dumbest and loudest radical minorities in order to put oil on the flames. They ,'politics & media', have become part of the problem, hardly offering any sound solutions and depicting every minor incident as a major event.

This is all quite retarded if were to look back upon the History of Europe. Inside Europe all major cities and even the country side is all made-up off mixed minorities. It has been so for at least half a century. Most people have integrated into local communities without any problem unless governments isolated them into minority ghetto's.

Indonesians, Spanish, Portuguese, South-Americans, , Polish, Turkish, Africans and many other world citizens have become integrate parts of Europe without any great difficulty. They have been contributing to the economic prosperity of Europe for decades, in many, many ways. It has been mostly government officials that have been squandering & corrupting taxpayers money through bad investments and lack of know-how. Many more millions have been lost by arrogant officials than that was ever spend on any & all refugees.

Europe is a culturally rich meltingpot, and needs to be proud of it's heritage and educate people as such. But so far Politicians & media have been doing a lousy job for the big wages they make. They are the ones that would all deserve major pay cuts.

The way America has contributed in creating social tension by typecasting minorities as stereotypes has also done no good at all to the process of mutual integration anywhere. This was clear in the colored /white issue as well as in the #metoo man/woman topic. It seems America at present can only export their own misery and chaos to other countries in the World. Destabilizing entire continents with their baseless geopolitical meddling.

It seems America has gone from a democratic role-model to a frustrated empire that is afraid to lose it's Global financial domination, within the last few decades.

Europe should be wiser and not blindly follow the US any-more or let the US direct any and all NATO actions as a Western expansion force. Intellect and long-term planning should prevail again, and not the taste of the day.

Europe should start their own culturally rich music channels to promote integration, instead of the Anglo-Saxon dominated music-industry at present that pushes gangsters, drugs & prostitutes. Create our own Hollywood Film-industry promoting European values. Not like the American Hollywood that at present is being dominated by the military industrial complex. Stop selling doom and gloom and a lack of creative vision for our common future. Be the future and get rid off career officials that play games with peoples future and keep us all stuck in antiquated ideas.

Europe needs decisive leadership to proceed into a healthy future. The economic tug-of-war within the Union is holding all member states back and creates it's own downfall. Create mutual respect for each-others cultures and stop meddling and selling arms to other countries outside the Union for sole geopolitical reasons. The Arrogance of the west can also be it's own downfall. So much is sure.

Do not just lock-up refugees you take in, in interment camps and years long procedures. Put them to work in fields on roads or hospitals to speed-up their integration without making them lose all dignity. Register them properly as you should have done from day one, and send economic refugees or criminals back without hesitation. Be a Union or be gone. We the People do not want your nonsense on our TV's and in our news every day.

We need you to do your work affective and in silence. You are no Pop-stars so stop behaving as such.

In order to create a sustainable healthy society all government departments including police, need to do their work transparent but in silence as much as possible, Do not constantly look at the media to validate your actions of the day. In order for the citizens of the Union to have their faith in politics restored, you all need to act and not talk and blame one another. Enough already. Be The Democratic Role-Model to the World again as you once were. Wise up already! Create solutions already! The World and mankind can no longer sustain your present many fuck-ups. We the people, need leaders we are able to believe in again.

Brussels at present is not cost effective and lacks any and all vision for a common future and is stuck in Economic tug of wars with other Nations, not respecting humanity as a whole. Not protecting citizens and consumers from greed or pollution. We need movies that depict something other than the retarded macho doom & gloom that comes out of Hollywood at present. It can be done if politicians stop being part of the problem, while selling futile solutions. We do not need more laws, but more common sense & education.

Shared responsibility is the key phrase in this all.

Bring a Union to the World & Unite Mankind.

16/ Is Democracy currently fighting a losing battle?

Democratic values are under threat almost everywhere around the Globe. People are being played against one another by government propaganda. Journalistic freedom has become more dangerous than ever and Civil-Rights are being threatened by corrupted politicians and justice systems like never before. What is going on?

Do we want war? Are we collectively so frustrated with our own lack of progression we seem to need to want to fight amongst ourselves? Everywhere?

The Turks are Threatening the Russians and Iraq. Russia feels threatened by European and NATO expansion so they join the fight? The Chinese are threatening Malaysia, Korea and Japan? Europe is turning into a right-wing Totalitarian political landscape? The US has a 170 bases outside it's own borders and threatens everybody?

Correct me if I'm wrong but, ...was the Military apparatus not intended as a deterrent from war? What happened? Did the Military Industrial Complex surpass it's own guidelines? Did the secret-service agencies become to intertwined with one another and turned into agents of chaos?

And the Police? To protect and serve? Serve what your puppet masters or the people working and paying taxes for your pay-check? Are you decreasing tensions in society or are you part of the problem steering society into civil-unrest or even civil-war? Are you cheap thrill-seekers or the fathers of the street and your communities?

These are all fair questions if we want to create any clarity and any sort of hope and vision for a combined collective future on this Planet of ours. Politicians can all go and visit expensive silly summits like the COP21, the G20 or G7, Davos, Bilderberg or whatever,..... They serve no purpose if there is no collective idea of where we want to go together.

The lack of progress by all World-Leaders is shameful and harmful to the entire Planet. There is NOT enough planet or atmosphere for us all if we let these failures continue. There won't be any gadget or app to save you from this foolishness. Slow down take a deep breath and stop talking each other into a frenzy. Not one of you is so important that your happiness needs to exceed that of the species. I do not care what your advisers say. You seem to suffer from tunnel-vision and a lack of imagination?

Most people in the world do not want anything to do with most of your sociopathic ambitions. Most people just want food & water friends and a roof over there head. If the so called ,'World Leaders', cannot provide that,... you should step aside and live out your perverted fantasies in private.

In an Industrialized World we cannot afford, the ancient colonial games to continue. Corruption is the biggest threat to healthy Democracies and our technical advancements are of such an order, that they do no longer allow for mistakes as made in past decades and centuries.

Is it a collective lack of courage by both people and leaders, why we do not make the steps necessary for progress? We have the know-how so much is clear. Now when will you captains of industry get behind the wheel and steer this ship or Vessel Earth into a future of regular progress instead of this up & down jojo ride. Your present actions are not sustainable in any scenario.

To be talking climate change together at the COP21 in Paris while at the other hand constantly threatening one another with wars in a Global arms-race is ludicrous. It's insane. It lacks any degree of intellect.

I do not care whether you are a Jew, Christian, Muslim, Buddhist, Atheist, Woman, Man, Gay or straight, you are all wrong, if you think there is any gain to be made by fighting one another over these differences. If you are not able to understand that, please go and fight and get it over with. Because stupidity does deserve to die.

This Planet is our school and if we do not find ways to better ourselves in body, mind & soul, we deserve to not go and become part of the bigger Universe. Than our history will end here on Earth and the story of mankind can be forgotten as a footnote.

Again, we do have the means and know-how to create rapid Global change in the way we facilitate our existence. If we however continue to let narrow-minded greedy little pervs. dictate our collective futures; than we are truly doomed. I can see a better future for us all. I can see it as clear as day. I can see healthy Democratic secular societies. So, why can't you? Are you caught up in small local, regional or religious little drama's? Are you all really still so childish to believe your truth is the only truth. Are you such junkies for adrenaline that you are willing to sacrifice you loved ones for some cheap thrills and short-term gains or profits?

Do you want big tits, dicks, lips, cars, houses or armies to show-off your stature? Have you all learned so little from past history that you think you can repeat the same mistakes without repent? You are wrong! No longer you can fight over countries and hide behind orders, borders and languages for what lies ahead. The Future is here, RightNow! Wise-Up Rise-Up This is about YOU2.

There are not too many people for this planet to stay sustainable. That is just a fear-mongering story. We can make everybody have clean water and a roof over their heads. It can be done. It only takes a refocus by all parties.

All Nation States have by now bought enough weapons to fight several WorldWars, so maybe now you can make the factories & Industry turn their attention on the creation of infrastructures for water, sanitation, shelter and the clean-up of our environment. Anyone who does not see that, needs to go check his doctor for medication.

WE THE PEOPLE can not afford corruption any longer.

Any further growth in Inequality will explode into unpredictable situations that will hurt us all! Everywhere. There is no, us or them. We need to make it work! Here & Now! We can make it work!   Here and Now!

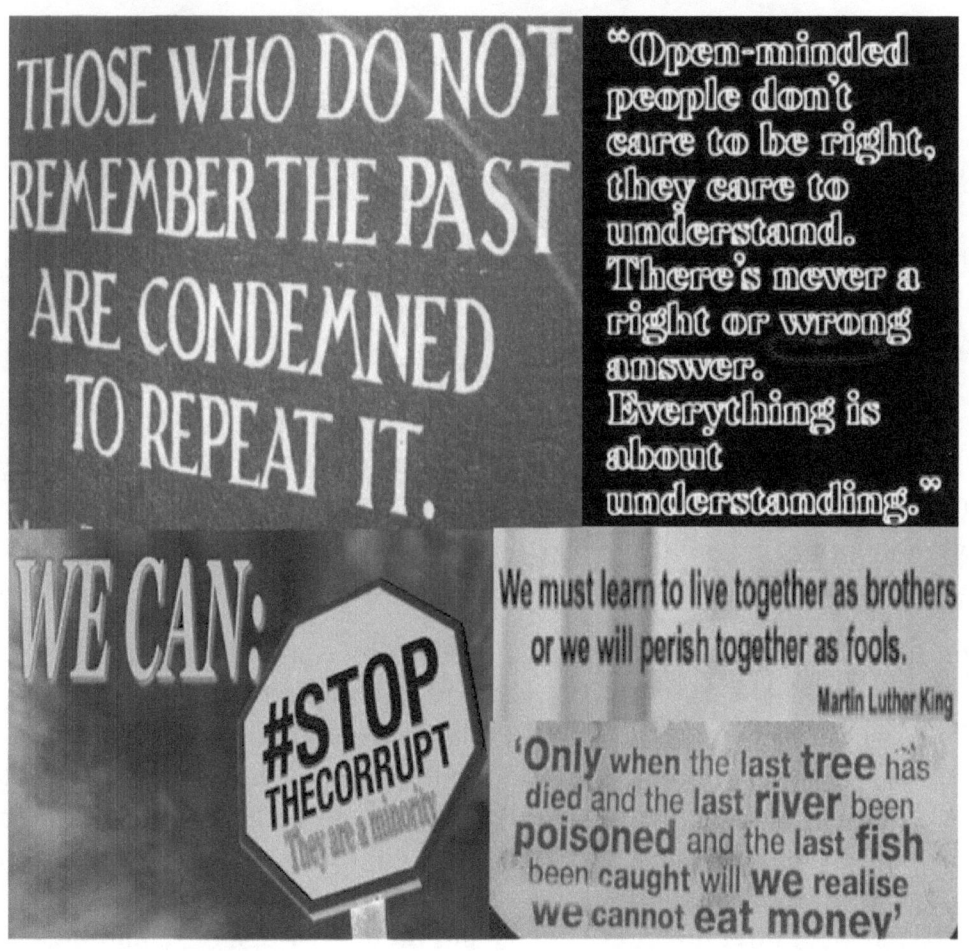

17/ Economic Growth is another word for:

Economic Warfare between Nations

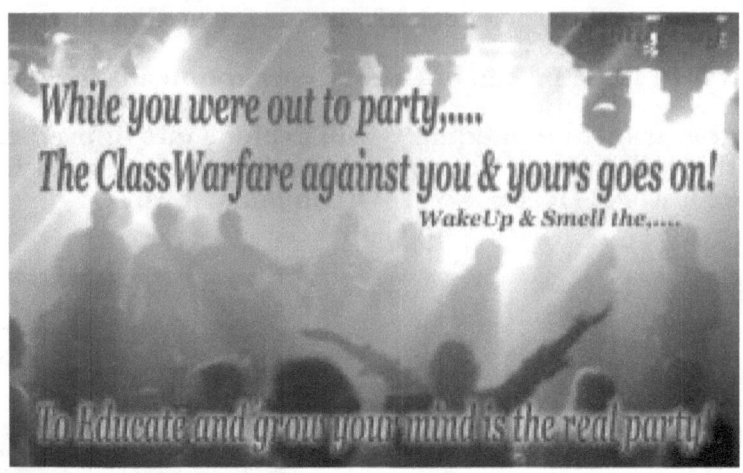

What is this foolish mantra called ,'Economic Growth', adopted by all so called World-leaders? These overpaid bookkeepers and accountants are selling-out & dragging humanity down into a World filled with Chaos, pollution & warfare. What the World and #WeThePeople need, is gradual economic growth and Infra-structures spread evenly across the Globe. At present economic paradigms are constantly shifting between Nations. It is a ongoing tug-off-war we are witnessing on a Global scale. Every Nations wants to be Top-Dog. This is truly the dumbest thing ever to be witnessed in our lifetimes!

Multinationals are already no longer limited by borders in their financial endeavours. They invest, produce and mine not bound by borders. However Governments are constantly worried about their ,'National Interests'. Can you see the contradiction here? So at present the corporate world wants to create a Global constitution that benefits primarily them and makes business dealings easier for them by cutting out the middle man from individual governments. The corporate world is rather frustrated with government officials and their slow response and lack in the decision making process. So, they move faster than all individual Governments and their civil servants in creating a Global new system of laws. They call them , 'Free Trade Zones'.

There are no Global Laws or Courts protecting citizens in their Civil-rights, Human-Rights or Consumer-Rights. Now the corporations want so called,' #free_trade_zones using some shady deals between the corporate World and individual Governments like the #TPP #TTIP #CETA #ISDS etc. etc. These deals would protect people even less and financial interests even more. It is so obvious, yet most people are kept in the dark over this dark looming future. News-Media do not do their job by properly informing people. So the Corporate Global take-over is a sneaky one.

Personally I would love to have a Global government, respecting the individual countries and their cultures and all people of the World. However,... at present this is not the case and we are all under threat by the shady ongoing deals and bribes between officials and lobbyists, to be drawn into another Global conflict. These guys do not seem to have the intelligence to grasp the understanding of our fragile planet and it's thin atmosphere providing us all with air to breath. These numb-nuts are willingly dealing away our collective futures. And do not believe they are smart just because they have expensive cars and even more expensive security teams,.... they are not! They are narrow-minded filthy-rich schmucks with tunnel-vision. All there expensive G8, G7, G20, Davos and Bilderberg meetings have proven this by now, by achieving nothing!

Life is not about gadgets, cars, luxury houses or fossil-fuels, it never was! These power-hungry idiots have kept the scientific evolution of our species back for at least one-hundred years. We could all be living in free & clean energy societies already! We could have created a better and cleaner environment for our children already! Yet we are kept back by Witches, Pimps & Pedophiles. We are kept divided over nonsense issues like gender, religion, color or country, and this renders us all, 'powerless'.

Even demonstrations have become a useless laughable tool for people to show their grievances. And even when Citizens and Police are fighting, those at the top are laughing all the way to the bank. Instead of coming together on the real issues of our time, we ventilate our frustrations by drinking, drugs and fighting. Instead of taking responsibility of our collective future we allow others to play us like pones and sheople.

So there it is. What will YOU DO?! When will YOU start to become a Global-Citizen and take responsibility for the future? Or will you just be another naïve stupid little barbiedoll or macho pimp/thug dumb dumb? Living a life directed by your masters of chaos, until they no longer need you and cast you aside like a filthy rag? Work until you die before getting an old-age pension, from cancer or whatever!? Or is that question beyond you? Too much maybe? Just asking.

But I am just alone, what can I do: I hear you ask. Well for one thing you could all come together on the important issues of our time, like #CleanEnergy #Pollution #HumanRights #ConsumerRights

It is up to you,...... up to you ALL! Freedom is not a given. It needs thinkers and do'ers. It needs real Union. Not the fake United States of Europe or America. Not some silly pop-song by another False-God from TV. Real People for our Real World. Anything else is just make-believe & false sentiment. Grow up! Become One! It can be done! YOU can do IT! This is your Planet! Make it Work! Economic Growth for All or no Growth at all!

Every gun that is made, every warship launched, every rocket fired signifies, in the final sense, **a theft from those** who hunger and are not fed, those who are cold and are not clothed. This world in arms is not spending money alone. It is spending the sweat of its laborers, the genius of its scientists, the hopes of its children.

Dwight D. Eisenhower

Do you remember those days? The days of CocaCola & Blue Jeans. Of family values and a rising middle class? The days of the Cold war crumbling under the images of people in the US enjoying a rising quality of live? What happened? Was it all a lie? It must have been a lie once we see the present Trans-National Corporations killing of the middle classes and their respective economies!

Free-Trade agreements like the TPP and the TTIP, CETA and others trying to openly undermine all forms of Democratic societies! They are blatantly attacking the already hollowed-out Democratic systems even further to get to some form of Corporate Technocratic Fascism!

It is like an all-out attack on humanity and human-rights itself. Extremism is on the rise on all sides, left or right-wing extremism, Christian, Muslim, Jewish or even on the gender issues! People are being played against one another like never before. It is shameful and lacks all common sense. We are all sub-divided into minorities and therefore not able to come together on matters that matter. It is like a road of no return and everybody just keeps on piling-on problems on top of one another like there already is no more tomorrow! It is fatalistic and points to a collective mental state of sickness.

The Military Industrial Complex is Globally arming itself at alarming rates and Governments are totally preoccupied with their Economic individual Dominance or survival. There is no Global vision now, at this time when we need it most.

Economic Warfare

Killing millions of people

All are focused on <u>economic growth</u> instead of <u>general well being or suffering</u>. None realize the futility of their endeavours. Politicians are also caught up in this useless capitalist game, dragging the World and all it's people down into an abyss. De Elite feel the people are becoming useless and can now be replaced with machines, so they feel the masses should perish or be massively reduced. These population reduction schemes have now been activated and will kill millions in the coming decade. Totally not necessary but we have lost empathy towards one another. Am I being to dramatic for you the reader maybe? Well,..good! I should be, because the clock just struck twelve!

In a little more than a hundred years we have succeeded in going from an industrial revolution to total confusion. Still think you are all so damned clever?! We could have slowly integrated growing wealth and better infra-structures into all economies worldwide, thereby creating growing quality off life for all! We could have used our growing technical know-how to implement better systems for <u>drip irrigation,</u> sanitation, production and waste recycling to benefit every country. Instead we, our Nations and leaders are choosing to fight over financial & Economic dominance and drag each other into proxy wars. Why don't you just all kill one another and try to start all over again. Or is that the idea?

Not to clever or creative are we now?! You must be very proud of your own intellect? No matter what side your on, this all amounts to nothing but Genocide on a Global scale. It drags down our collective evolution and is downright dumb. But hey Fight-On by all means at least we can only fuck up this world. And that's no Science-Fiction!

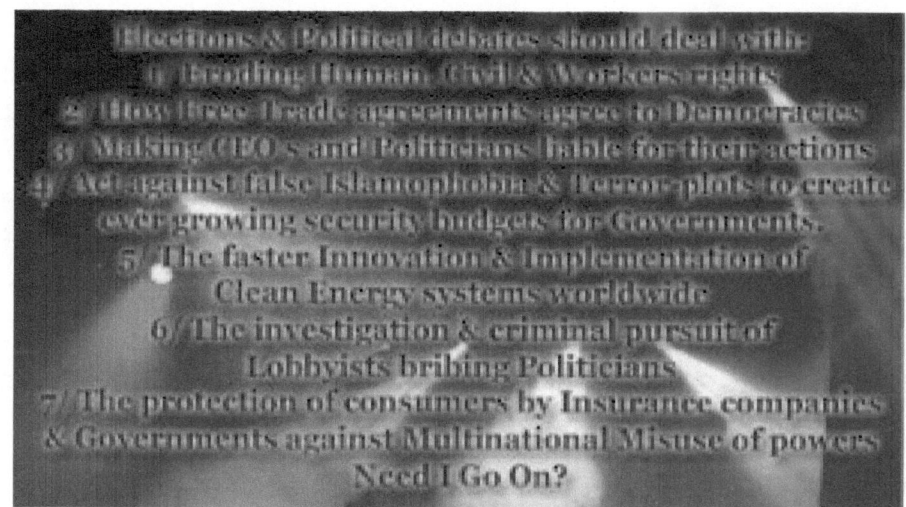

Elections & Political debates should deal with:
1/ Eroding Human, Civil & Workers rights
2/ How Free Trade agreements agree to Democracies
3/ Making CEO's and Politicians liable for their actions
4/ Act against false Islamophobia & Terror plots to create ever growing security budgets for Governments.
5/ The faster Innovation & Implementation of Clean Energy systems worldwide
6/ The investigation & criminal pursuit of Lobbyists bribing Politicians
7/ The protection of consumers by Insurance companies & Governments against Multinational Misuse of powers
Need I Go On?

19/ Mixing The Planet

(Tribal Fears & Confusions.)

The most ignorant and fearful people in the World always hide within large groups of tribes or other compositions. It doesn't really matter for these lesser educated folks. As long as they can find some sense of safety within any group of people, being it religious, gay, biker, black, white or otherwise. It is of-course a false sense of security they find, but in many dangerous parts of our planet, most do not see another choice.

It takes a lot of courage to shape your life as an individual, living amongst so many fearful people in this still very uncertain World we live in. It takes real courage to become a **Global Citizen!**

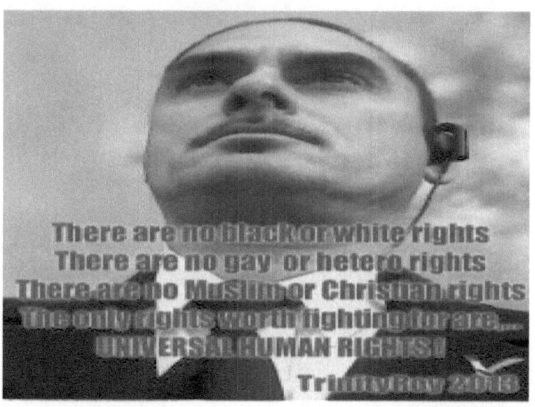

There are no black or white rights
There are no gay or hetero rights
There are no Muslim or Christian rights
The only rights worth fighting for are:
UNIVERSAL HUMAN RIGHTS!
TribuRey 2016

We also see mankind constantly repeating historically known mistakes over & over again. This proofs our slow learning curve in these matters. The moment an individual feels threatened or afraid in any given situation they fall back into the old family or tribal oriented groups. These groups often turn out to actually be more vulnerable to manipulation by market driven forces and/or power hungry despotism.

Most groups centre around ideas & myths of purity or religious correctness, putting their ideologies forth as the only truth, sticking to their guns out of sheer lack of courage and education.

Throughout Human History this stereotypic behaviour has cleverly been used by Colonial conquerors, Tyrannic rulers, and economic marketing forces, in order to manipulate and divide people away from finding harmony and peace or even to keep people from rising-up as one. Keeping people confused, divided and frustrated has become a business skill. Especially when research in the second half of the 20th Century showed that frustrated consumers, consume more. This conclusion was summarized as: , **'Greed exceeding need'**. This same knowledge is used by Governments to keep their internal economies going when exports are slowing down. It makes their own citizens buy more than they need out of feelings of frustration or a general lack of happiness. It is the same as an unhappy woman going on a shopping spree just to fill her frustrated unhappy life or soul with just about anything. Or people trying to eat away their lack of satisfaction. Or Drug use, or binge drinking! These are all obvious flaws in our modern societies, that are cleverly used and maintained to make money from misery.

This is why we stay racists, nationalists, fascists, warmongers, extremists and fanatics. This is why we are still so divided after centuries of repeating the same mistakes over & over again.

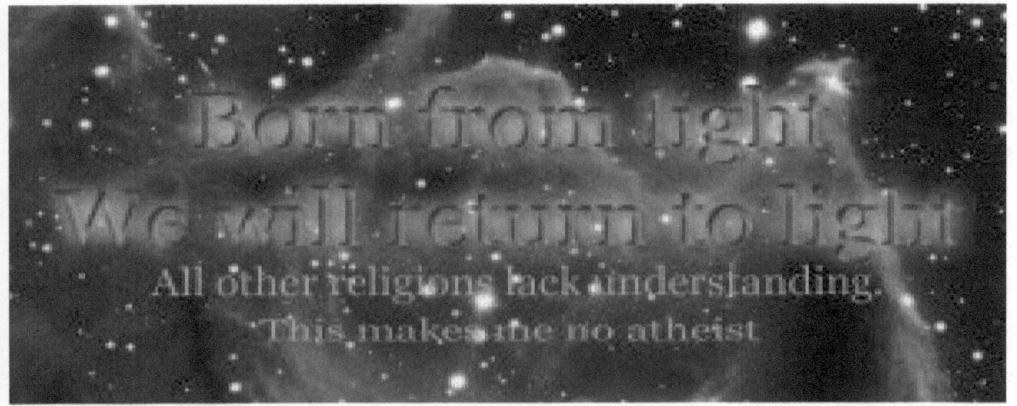

Born from light,
We will return to light
All other religions lack understanding.
This makes me no atheist

I believe we as a species are and have always been of mixed origin. Mixed as we came from space as micro-organisms travelling on meteorites. Or mixed as we spread-out over this planet as its first explorers adapting to different circumstances, everywhere we travelled. It is ,'**too late to separate**', It has always been. We just do not seem to understand this fact and hide the truth out of individual fears and such.

And within all this Black & White talk, the,.. Muslim, Jew, Buddhist or Christian talk, we seem to forget the millions of people that have been born from ,'mixed', parents. What about them?! Are they not worthy? To what group do they belong? The Global Bastards or Muds Foundation, maybe? This is about as stupid and funny as the whole idea of segregation. It is as dumb as us waving flags and raising borders. It is as dumb as thinking people are simply gay or heterosexual. As dumb as getting stuck in, ´us or them´, dogmas. The gradations in which people differ from one another go way further than just gay, heterosexual, man, woman, black, Asian or white!? These are just simplifications for lazy minds. I personally see myself as part of a group of courage's individuals in full respect of each others differences.   **I am a Global Citizen**

As an example I would like to focus on Gay Rights. Gay or LGTB rights movements have created their own PrideParades Worldwide. And as such they , 'as well as Black or Woman-rights-activists', have given way to extremist counter movements and actions. If they would have been smart enough to stick to the Equal Rights and Human Rights issues, we possibly could have made more progress faster than we are doing at present. It is a very Corporate-Industrial and Hollywood-American way to put minorities forth as stereotypes. This however mostly does not benefit the goal in advancing all rights for all people everywhere! Therefore I call for the creation of People Pride Parades. Parades that facilitate all minorities and cultures. That would make me proud!

Narrow-minded concepts just slowdown the entire evolution of mankind and perpetuate wars and conflicts. They keep us all from reaching our full potential and make us stay stuck in retarded backward mindsets. These ways of the old, create wars, pollute our environment and cost fortunes that could have been spend much better and more cost effective.

The modern day profits, profit primarily from inequality, not from growing equality or prosperity. The sociopathic money sharks & speculators mostly lack a broader vision or compassion for those that are adversely touched by their market tradings. They just want short-term & quick big profits for themselves or their shareholders, no matter how many suffer or die from their actions. For these financial-elite there are no borders no more and neither are they ever legally properly prosecuted as they should be, for their often criminal behaviour.

Anyway, welcome to this planet YOUman, full of flaws and slow learning curves. This planet creating life from it's constant fight between fire, water & gravity. This planet situated in the Milkyway inside a fast ocean of mixed Milkyways inside an even faster ocean that is the Universe. Now open your minds you silly primates, learn & evolve so that maybe one day you can reach the full human potential and fly amongst the stars. But 1st you will all have to make it work, ... here on Earth!

20/ Debt creation as a tool to enslave people & Nations

The Western World has been doing it for over a 100 years. They at first started with the developing countries, giving them loans knowing they would only be able to pay the yearly interest if that at all. Ensuring this way that these countries would not achieve economic independence. In the meantime western subsidized products would flood these countries, killing of small local farmers and entrepreneurs. The colonial games of the financial elite did not end there, because attached to the loans were stipulations given rights to the lenders to mine precious metals, oil and such. Hereby ensuring the legalized theft from these countries. This is how it was and is done!

In our modern times these enslaving methods go even further. At present these methods are being used to enslave all people regardless of race or color and even <u>entire Nations.</u> The ECB, IMF and <u>World Banks</u> have become more powerful than any individual Democracy. <u>All being ruled by the BIS in Basel</u> This was also the case with Greece where the loans were giving knowingly to overextend Greece so it would not be able to pay these back, this in order to force <u>Greece to Privatize their countries assets</u>. Any and all forms of election of civil representatives has thereby been reduced to a farce and circus for the camera's only. Bread and Games, nothing more.

Economic interests have been lifted way above the welfare of the people. Farmers smartness by well educated elected officials did do nothing to prevent that. These officials have been selling out our collective environment, health and quality of life as a whole. They sold out our sanity for short term profit models. The people were in the meantime kept in the dark and were informed as little as possible of what was going on. With the aid of the media the shortcomings of our political and corporate leaders were downplayed. The lack of vision for our common future has been cleverly been obscured and any Democratic model for the 20st Century, hollowed out. At present nobody believes their sales pitches any-more, yet nobody has any idea how to start to change without falling into complete chaos and disarray.

In the meantime people and entire Nations are being played against one another, in order to keep frustration at an all-time high, so the CEO's of the Big Industrial Conglomerates will be able to instate and force their fascist ideas upon us. They do this using Hollywood, Disney, MTV and Wargames to achieve their goal.

Woman with ugly fake nails, tits, lips and hair extension in plastic tight suits and guys in plastic expensive cars using dick enlargers and steroids never ever being satisfied, no matter what! And we are surprised the use of anti-depressants is ever increasing? Even the Global increase of the middle-classes in this way will create more problems than solutions for our species and planet. Logistically we could have achieved way more advancement, were it not for the lack of willingness of our leaders to admit to their shortcomings. Instead they are all playing retarded backward territorial games of economic dominance.

The entire World and mankind could have already been supplied with sanitation, fresh drinking water and general education were it not for these nitwits. The total development of our species has been slowed down & hampered by these failed overpayed bookkeepers.

In the meantime the new liberal right extremist train of thought, dualism and polarization makes people lose empathy towards their own, will only increase cruelty and suffering on a Global scale. No thanks to the in no way creative yet always macho movies & series coming out of Hollywood, more often than not sponsored by the arms-industry. What a shame Democracy could not have stayed with the image of Coca-Cola and blue jeans, maybe than our species would have still stood a change. At present the nearby future is showing an ever increasing frighten perspective which will probably cost the lives of many millions of people. We have to stop being played against one another, no matter what tribe, religion or heritage. We will have to start to make it work together. We have the know-how and technology to feed Each & every person on the planet using clean energy. It is the fossil fuel barons that kept us from developing as we should have. We need to stop the socio-paths, cocaine junkies & paedophiles, dragging us down any further into oblivion. All hands to the helm are needed to achieve this. No matter who, what or where you are! This World is run by Fisherman, Farmers, Construction workers, Technicians, Doctors, Fathers, Mothers, Brothers & Sister. Not by Bankers, Insurers or Politicians so much should be clear by now. Civil servants will need to start serving the public again and stop playing games like some useless popstar or actor. It can be done!

21/ Insurance companies & Governements

on the wrong side of the Law?

So who is the customer?

Who are civil servants to our citizens?

According to the Neo-Liberal standards, those that do not work or lack financial powers, do not matter in society. The flagrant dehumanization is in full swing in most developed and underdeveloped countries. While each country is forced to fight for its own economic survival, Globally this translates in rising tensions, war and suffering.

Looking at Insurance companies makes this evident quite easily: Now the customer gives power to the insurance companies by means of their monthly premiums. These translate into billions of revenue for companies that should not make profits from suffering.

Look at healthcare as an example; The power given to the insurance companies could be used as leverage to put pressure on big pharmaceutical companies to make better and cheaper medicinal cures . The insurers should represent the interests of their clients. Pharmaceutical companies are already Government funded and /or subsidized for their research projects?! Instead they are bribed and bought by these same companies into selling you the most expensive and not always healthier ,'cures'. These same companies are also not held responsible for the burden they inflict on the environment, from their discarded produce.Why do insurance companies put the burden on the customer and not pressure Big Pharma for better, healthier deals? Isn't that what we pay them for?

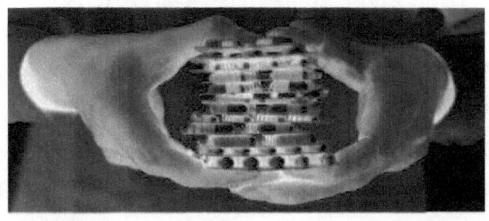

This is a completely out of balance situation that needs immediate fixing. Who should fix that? Legislation. Your Government officials. Do they? No, they do not, because they are being bribed by corporate lobbyists. Just imagine if all these wasted funds would be allocated into Human Welfare? This would make a huge difference on all our societies.

It seems our overly well paid government officials are not doing their job in protecting their citizens or the environment. They pretend to be well educated but are selling away basic human rights like they would selling a bunch of cows or pigs. Farmers smartness can not be applied to World leaders, so much is clear. It will lead us all onto a path of mutual destruction, only to be covered up with yet another self-inflicted war.

Now most people have already lost their faith in Insurances or Governments but they lack options to change or better the future. These options should be presented by for example the UN or WHO, but guess what, these have also been bribed and lobbied to submission by Multinationals.

These institutions cost a lot and do not deliver enough!

Now what should be done???

We should criminalize cross border infringements of environmental or Human & Civil Laws. CEO's and Government officials need to be prosecuted. And not be able to swap places every four years to continue their crimes. Where is the International court of Justice or @ICJ in these matters? Corporate person-hood is a loophole in the law that grants powers to companies, but let's their CEO's avoid liability.

We need to stop playing catch-up with this ever growing lack of morality in leadership now!

We have to know-how, but seem to lack the courage. We fight more with one another than with those that want to become rich quick, killing of millions of people doing so. Filthy rich is no empty term. For every person getting rich quickly, many must die.

Now I do not have a problem with income inequality, as long as it serves sound systems. At present however it needs to be addressed rather sooner than later. YOU owe it to your children and yourselves to fight for what is right. Your gadgets and insecure infighting has no purpose and needs to be refocused onto those that have lost all morality and have become nothing more than mentally sick socio-paths. This is the way to get to a once again prosperous future for mankind.

Educate each other, grow your minds, harmonize your souls. It can be done!

We will still be confronted with natural disasters and Global tensions on our way to a better future, but hopefully less problems of our own creation. Apply new found technology onto cleaner energy, better cures & drugs, and ,'cradle to the grave', systems of production. Do away with the Lords of war, Corrupt Bankers and Insurances. Do away with these mentally sick paedophiles and their unfounded arrogance. No more Devils advocates that prolong cases to make more money for those that already make sickening amounts, while so many suffer. It can be done! We have the means but seem to lack the brains and courage.

I call upon the law student worldwide to do what is right. Prosecute the hell out of these criminals.

Find ways to change their ways or throw them in jail. Stop pursuing small criminals or drugs dealers who are more often than not, just forced into bad situations by the bigger thieves at the top and civil injustice. These are the old ways and lack all validity. We see through these old ways and need to educate all our brothers and sisters about them. Do it now, or shut the ,.... up when federal fascism is what rules our world in the nearby future. Stop playing with your phones,... use them and your social networks. Spread the word and take positive action.

It can be done! Real food, real fun, real life for real people, it can be done!

22/ Failing Global Leadership.

We only have to look at the present state of the World to know this is true. Instead of spreading Democracy, Equality and general well-being these so called ,'Civil-Servants', have only bettered their own pay and not shown any real leadership. After hundreds of major World-wide conferences like the G7, G20, Davos, etc, etc, extravagant expensive travels, Hotels, diners and of-course security expenses, they have accomplished close to nothing.

Not since the second World-war have so many people been displaced (50 million+). The environment nearing complete destabilization with ,'again', hardly any actual results to show for their efforts. The only results we can witness are the many civil and other wars and the massive arms-race that is taking place Globally. Corruption and the drug trade as well as human trafficking are more rampant than ever. Thanks for nothing I would say! When will you start making money from the creation of peace?

Water, sanitation, homes and infra-structure for all, there's your work cut out for you!

Since the start of the war against terrorism, what we have seen is an incredible rise of this so called terrorism. Again thanks for nothing! Create the problem & Sell the solution!? Our News-Media has become a propaganda tool for governments and big-corporations. Our fellow-citizens such as Police & soldiers have been gradually morphing into Governments pansies, becoming more & more aggressive against their own fellow citizens instead of serving those that pay their wages, The People!

Just following orders?? I don't think so! It is a lack of civilization and intelligence.

It is not remembering the lessons of History, obeying your countries constitution and not protecting civil-liberties. It is a shameful showing of a lack of knowledge and general interest in the well-being of fellow human beings. This Neo-Liberal, Capitalist, extremist, detachment is dehumanizing and sets people apart. It definitely does not bring them together, so much is sure.

Why are we paying these Politicians such high wages when they provide so little results? Why should they be protected with so costly security, when they don't do the same for you?
You need to think about these issues because they concern the health of your Democracies, your children and yourselves. We are loosing our collective focus point and are derailing our societies like a bunch of complete crazy lunatics. We can no longer let the actions of a minority of mentally sick psychopaths dictate the future of the majority. We have the means to create a prosperous World for all, sanitation and infrastructures that can serve all. It is just a few retarded old minds that want us to believe otherwise. And ,'they', are using all the means at their disposal, such as media corporations & Films, as well as games to corrupt our minds.

If needed we need to bring out the pitchforks and get rid off these failures to re-establish a healthy focus on the future of humanity again. And we better be quick about it. I believe these deranged mentally sick elite want to decimate the entire Global population, by *creating as much random chaos as possible*. They will do this with wars, the spread of viruses, the domination of water and food and any other way they can.

They have already begun their war on the middle-classes and could soon spread them to every & anybody anywhere. No matter what your religion or culture is, this is no game no more.

This is a fight for all our survival now!

There is no need for recessions, there can only be growth if only we leave the old ways behind. The ways of starting Global conflicts every 50 years to create another economic boom, with riches for a few and suffering for the many are to be over. We the people have let ourselves become divided like never before in human history. It is outrageous what is happening at this time. It serves no purpose and can only lead to mass devastation of humans and nature. It is not needed!

Now,... if we can not <u>do away with corruption</u> and find common ground, than it is probably better to all go out and shoot each other right now. If we cannot understand that we need to guide our present frustrations against those that created them, and not each other,..... Than we probably deserve every war we get. If we rather talk about sex, food and the most superficial TV programs instead of what really matters to your future and that of your children,... Than your love is empty and useless. We need to share responsibility for everything we do! It is OK to love your country, flag, city, tribe or whatever local or religious group you want to belong to. What is not OK, is not to not see the common ground we all share, as in being on one planet together. This can no longer be tolerated. These are the ways of old Machiavellian, Roman, Nazi & Stasi teachings and they are outdated. These are not the ways you want your children to inherit from you. You need to become better role-models and do away with these silly retarded games. If Democracy cannot provide some real leadership, I myself would prefer a dictatorship to a Democracy. Because a bad dictator can more easily be toppled by it's people. *Democracies just slowly turn to fascism and bleed to death if not kept healthy by it's people.*

You Cops & Soldiers need to start thinking again and represent the needs of your people and not your governments or big corporations. 'I was just following orders', has been proven by history to not do any good and result in mass suffering and killings of your own brothers & sisters.

You soldiers & police need to wake up and turn your frustrations onto those that create these frustrations, not your fellow citizens & human beings. This is the only way to create better societies to live in. A better quality of life for all. It can be done and needs to get done. The only good fight is a fight for Civil & Human - Rights. If this needs a radical toppling of leadership, so be it. The builders, doctors, bakers, farmers and such will continue to hold society together as they always have done. Those pariah's such as insurers, bankers and stockbrokers can go fck themselves after doing so much harm to the World and people in general. They deserve no piety no more. Let's get some sanity back on TV and onto our streets. Go out and talk with each other without making it into small drama's and petty-fights, like the ones we were sold on TV and in Films from Hollywood. Don't be aggressive, show some class and Intelligence and be a part of humanity. Point your anger towards those who deserve it, not your neighbours. Depict the future as you want to see it, not as ,'they', are selling it to you. Do away with those shallow macho brains & muscles, brothers & Sisters and become part of the solution. It can be done and the sooner the better. You don't have to be on TV to be. On the contrary, you just have to be alive and educate yourself and get better. That is all you need to do!

23/ Global Polarization in the 21st Century

Come on people, how stupid are we really? No please do not answer to quickly. Please stop and think for once in your short petty-full lives.

After the second world-war the modern world went through a period of relative peace and developments. We created an image of Democracy that was selling itself around the world. An image of water, food, housing and clothing for everybody. Basic Human Rights as a positive catalyzing narrative that pushed the entire Scala of Global developments including capitalism, forward. It made Russia come about and even made China join the race forward.

And now, what happened? Who happened? The forces of good have turned evil for all intents and purposes. The Elite has detached completely from the working-class and Industry seems to be working more & more against Humanity than for it? Even the Politicians are turning against their own electorates and species. Sure we came forth from a conquering species of colonialists, but this present mental sickness goes way beyond those original outsets and goals.

As a species we are falling apart at the seams. We are polarizing on so many different issues that all logic seems forgotten.

Look at the Arab-Spring that became an Arab-Fall. In most Arab countries now they are divided in factions and tribes as in olden days. Egyptians, Libyans, Syrians, Iraqi, Somali, Sudanese and now, Ukrainians fighting each-other while their soils are being polluted and fossil wealth is being robbed from under their feet.

The Ukrainians could have all been rich if they would have been smart enough to play out both the EU, US and Russia. Now their stupidity resulted in them killing one another.

All are being played in games by Industrial conglomerates. All are being played and divided so others can make gain and profits over the corpses of those that are being killed by random acts of stupid hate sentiments, induced by these same corporations and their puppets.

In the meantime all National governments are being played into debt and thereby submitted to the will of Financial-Institutions not scrutinized by any law or Democratic supervision.

Why were tensions being played up between Arab and African countries? Why are tensions being played up between the neighbours China, Japan, Taiwan & Vietnam? Why are tensions being played up between Russia, Europe and their regional neighbours? Who is benefiting? Why did the News Media lose all their journalistic integrity? Why indeed!?

It is not always as obvious as an all-out war, but it's just as devastating. It will set the total Global development back for at least another century, 'again'. It will further pollute our environment and create unspeakable suffering for billions of people, as it is doing already right now! It lacks any form of intelligence as is merely based on sick egocentric arrogance based on nothing but failures and short-term profits. It is shameful, and *all those so called G20, UN or other summits are useless*. Our so called 'leaders', act as famous popstars or actors in some silly cheap hollywood script. They drive around feeling more important than their electorates and feel the need to be protected, leaving their people to stand and fall alone in their struggle for a better life.

It seems everything in Politics and Industry needs to be protected by expensive security systems, while the people are left to fight on their own without the means to do so! No actual Human-Consumer or any Basic-Rights. They are being sold-out!

Even the Justice systems in our Democratic Nations have been corrupted by Industry. Lobbyists are targeting our representatives relentlessly and bribes are common goods everywhere. I would install a , 'cordon sanitair', around Brussels, Washington, Peking and Moscow to fight off these corporate predators. Lawyers get rich fighting of claims and even they no longer serve true justice. Even some judges have given in to the pressure of governments and Industry and became corrupted, no longer following good-sense or logic. The people do no longer know where to turn to for actual justice and become bitter and frustrated. And as a result of all this infighting we now see a rise of civil-unrest all over the World. Thanks for nothing I would say. Thanks for destroying our collective hopes of positive Global developments. Thanks for destroying our faith in Human kindness and turning it into shared baseless hate. Thanks for nothing. Nothing at all.

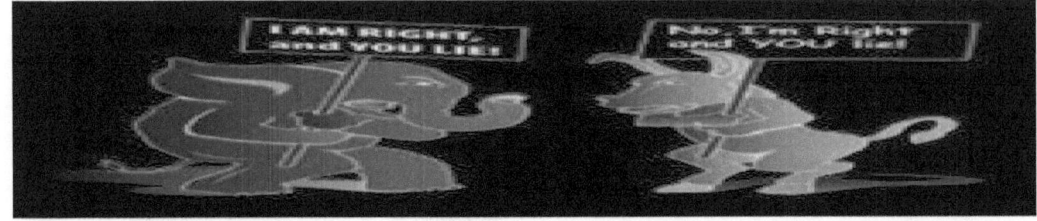

<u>Stop to fight each-other</u> so some can make big profits over the backs of your dead bodies. Wise-up all you people everywhere. We must make a change and call these companies to justice no matter who they are, or where they operate. That is what the International Tribunal in The Hague should be used for. But they probably also lack the balls or legal parameters.

I am sure we could make leaps forward into creating a better World for all, with the technology we presently posses. However if we remain stuck in old-fashioned colonialists war-games, we will surely perish. Maybe it will be a slow demise or a sudden bang and it's over, but we cannot stay on our present track without paying the consequences.

We have the tools and means to change the World in a prosperous place for all. We will have to get rid of those that have been holding back our collective evolution for the last 200 years (if not more). This is not about any single government or company. This is not about pointing fingers and putting the blame. This is about finding a common ground and basis from where we can all work on a shared future, together. I do not care how intelligent or important you believe yourselves to be.

This is about leaving behind those narrow-minded Industrial fascist ideas of the 20th Century and going forward in creating basic sanitation and infra-structures for all of mankind. It can be done if we just *do away with the little gray-suited, cocaine sniffing, cowardly paedophiles* that are determining our future at present. They need not to be protected any longer and fall in-line or be done away with.

For the sake of Us All and our children, we will need to engage in this fight for good, Now! This is not some common cold we fight of with some pills. This needs to be a grass-roots movement wherein we all need to come together and put our petty differences of creed, colour and religion aside. When the people are No longer divided, the Elitist manipulators and their doctrines are rendered powerless and power will come back in the hands of the people, for the people! It can be done, but only if we STOP to fight one another. No opinion is more important than the next, unless it benefits everybody everywhere. There is no left or right side that is primarily right. We have the technology, now all we need is the common sense to do it.

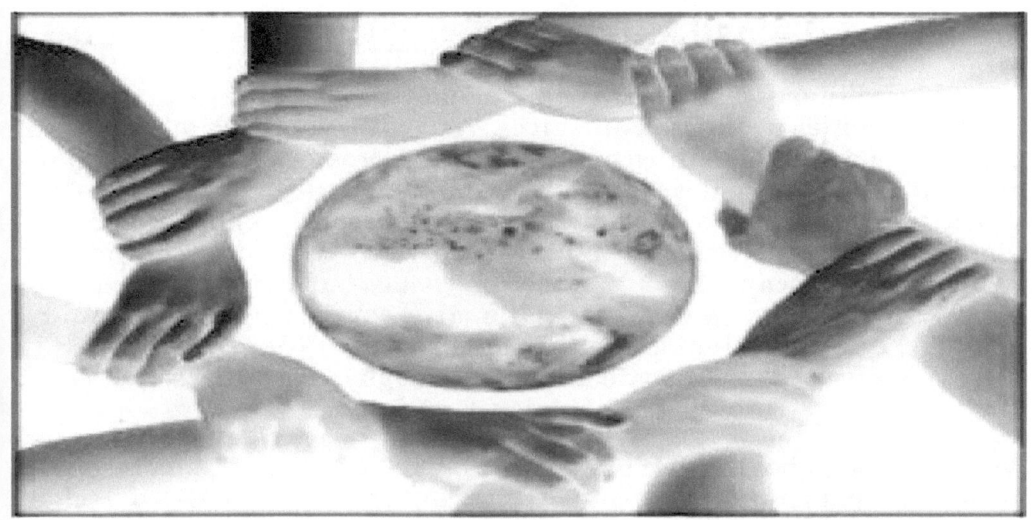

STOP being sheep divided in herds by bad shepherds. STOP hiding behind flags, languages and borders that do not actually exist, but by our own creation. One Planet, One People. It is not so hard to do if you think about it. Soldiers, Police, Farmers, Carpenters, Mothers, Fathers, Brothers & Sisters You are One! *A divided people is a weak people.* So get it on and learn to live together, because for every bit of suffering prolonged by yourselves, YOU yourselves will pay the price, as sure as the World will keep on turning.

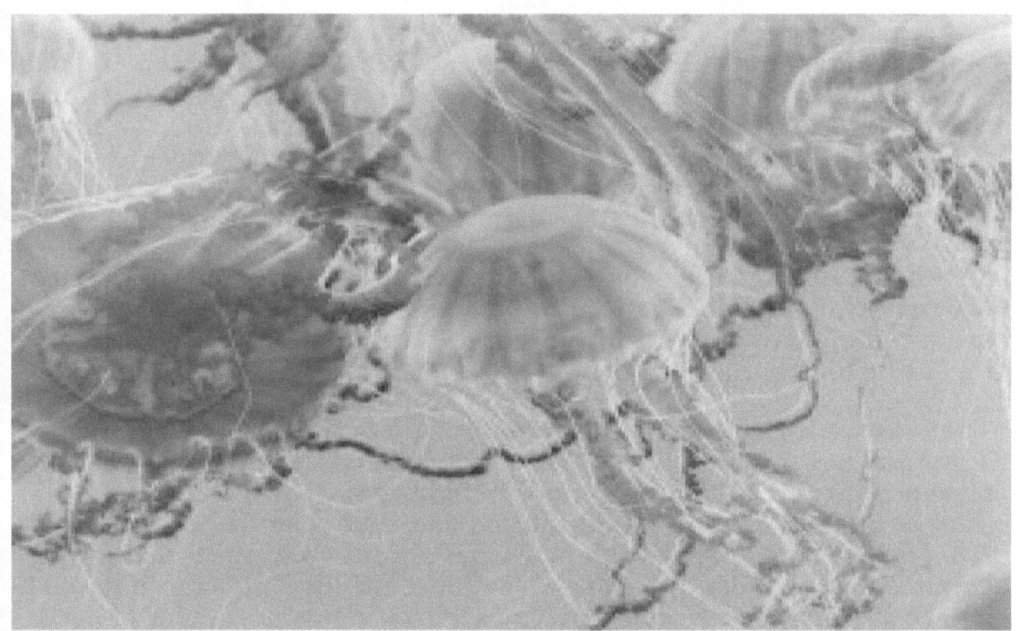

24/ Small Minds in a Great Universe.

Damn how silly are we people? We are all playing silly little games within silly little realities we created ourselves. We are playing each other within tiny little fantasies and little communities. We create stories on the spot and, than we start to believe these short-minded hardly creative fantasies. We act upon these self-created fantasies. They become us and we become them. And, not surprisingly on top of our little self-created realities; there are always some people that play the same games but on a larger scale. So here we are living personal, local, national or continental realities. And all of these are, 'small-minded'. They do no justice to our real potential. It's the way we presently still think and imagine our futures, that is holding our Human-Family back.

We as a species hold within our genetic make-up the possibility for the divine. This planet was just planned as a giant school for us all to develop and prosper. However we are stuck in ancient colonial states of minds and it seems we are not able to shake our old ways. No matter how far we have developed technically due to the Industrial revolution. We are still using our minds as retarded Neanderthals. We are no masters of our own emotions or even aware of the fact that we are all guided by mere chemical signals. We believe to be smart and then connect the image of smartness to some primal idea of alpha-males & females. This than again clears the way to stay divided and dominated by some skinny paedophile dudes in grey suits .

Talking for myself; I do not belong to any single group of people, unless it's a group of real individuals called People. I am a Global Citizen and will not be reduced to anything less by anyone's stupid concocted little game. I am here to live and learn. I am here to develop my senses and grow into a worthy entity allowed and able to go beyond the atmosphere and boundaries of this Planet. I am and will be! No matter what the matter, it being flesh or light itself. I Am.

And I am, because We are. Ubuntu. I am, because We are. This is the most basic reality of all. This is the truth to the matter, no matter what. There are no winners or losers in this matter. We Humans either cross the finish-line together as one, or not even make it to the finish-line at all.

There are only two entities or forces at work in the known Universe. Matter and anti-matter, as in light & darkness. These two forces are the basic make-up and all matter is made of light. What the darkness or anti-matter consists off, is still largely unknown to our scientific community. That is why we still are wondering whether our Universe is actually shrinking or expanding. But I am here now! I am alive and conscious so I will have to learn and grow my total awareness of this particular being. It is not enough to waist my life, by just eating and converting', as some simple fungi or bacteria.

And that is what it all boils down to; To not become trapped in small minded creations that keep our souls captured in unnecessary agony and suffering. That make us repeat historic mistakes over and over again. To not drag ever more generations of our own, into useless repeats of old mistakes.

So pull your minds out of the gutters of gloom and doom. Create a better future for your children and take back this shared responsibility from any so called leaders or sellers of false insurances and securities. We need to, 'at least ', take back the possibility of choice. We need to all finally start to, 'Act Local – Live Global'. The only right or actual responsibility is shared responsibility. We will Live and prosper together, or we will perish together. Leaving behind nothing,.... Nothing at all. We could become a dead-zone in a Galaxy of life. So let's generate the right spirit and put in the right effort into becoming the true beings of light we really are. Let's slowly begin our voyage and return into the lap of our creator as fully grown self-supporting entities of pure light. No longer bound and restraint to a single planet. That is when we will have become truly an Adult Humanity. Truly aware and conscious.

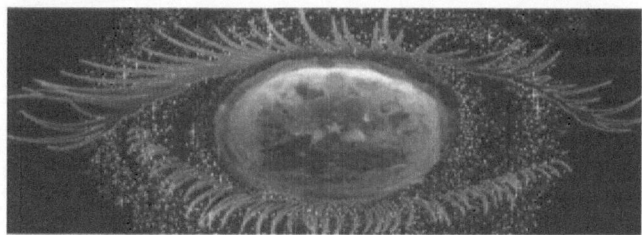

You are both Water & Fire, to be narrowed down to a choice of either is to not respect life itself. Life would not have come about without either of those two. And both are needed for our continued survival. So wake-up and see, smell, taste and feel, all that is around you. The more you grow, the greater the joy. And that is no empty promise.

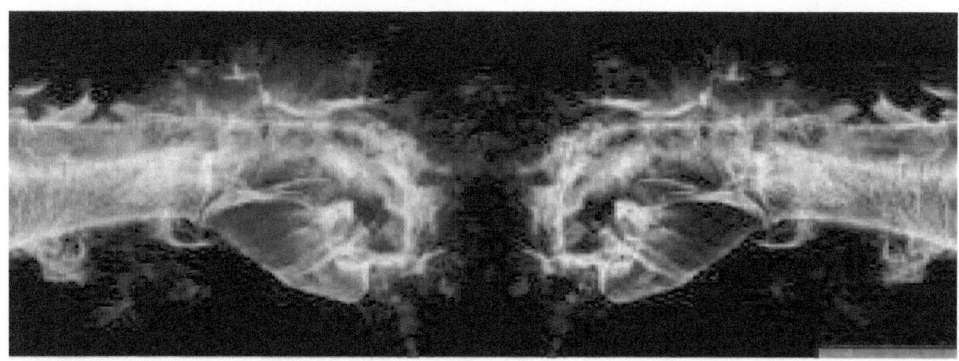

25/ Eat, Fuck, Fight and go to War.

(The father The Son & The Holly Spirit)

How can this scripture be translated into a modern equivalent meaning?

Personally I would translate it as such: Water + Fire = Life & Creation.

As we are born on Planet Earth it would explain a lot. This Planet would never have brought Life if Fire and Water wouldn't have struck a balance here! The tense balance between those old adversaries has given our planet a breathable atmosphere and is the origin of all life as we know it.

So, If Fire is the Father and Water is the Son; then the resulting Holy Spirit would be Life itself.

In our known human History, we people have still not mastered our living languages and ways in which we communicate. We have and are still looking for the right ways and words to express ourselves ever better. The resulting consequences in our present modern times are a lot of misunderstandings between people and their respective Nations and/or religions.

The biggest problem in solving these misunderstandings is the fact that there are so many so called political-leaders, priests and their followers, pretending that their believes are better than any other. That they know or understand our past and future better. The fact that most people still cannot admit that they are not as smart as they pretend to be, it is what is being used against to keep us under the thumb and forever divided & dominated by a minority of the filthy rich. It is our collective mistake for not taking responsibility for our combined future and that of our children. We are ,'all', to blame!

Instead of learning from our two original parents, Water & Fire, who showed us how two violent opponents can live and create together, we continue to play silly little games. These games resulted in sick over regulatory-systems run by small-minded bureaucrats in ever growing radicalised societies.

We pay insurance companies to carry our individual responsibilities and we instate ministers, queens and presidents to take care of our collective responsibilities. What else would we not like to take care of ourselves? Well that doesn't really matter, now does it? Let's keep it simple and *Eat, Fuck, Fight and go to War*. And afterwards the remaining survivors can cry on each others shoulders and tell stories of stupidity bravery and courage. Stories about brothers killing brothers and Neighbours killing neighbours.

This is why we are so slow in developing as a species. Even with all our smart-gadgets individually we are mostly still quite retarded. We lack individual insight and knowledge in our own actions and the resulting problems. That is why our respective societies are in constant turmoil and chaos.

We need to start to carry our individual burden of responsibilities towards ourselves and the people around us. We need to develop from player-haters into keepers & creators. We need to stop to blame others and any simple minority for our shortcomings. It is as the fornicator and alcoholic screaming blasphemy at the gay and such. Those that are without sin, should throw the first stone. That means that most of all people anywhere do not have the right to throw stones at anybody for any reason. But if you are too stupid to control your fire within and your individual frustrations, than you probably do not deserve to be cleansed with water nor blessed with peace and harmony.

So we need to individually and collectively start to take care of ourselves and those around us. *aCT Local - tHINK gLOBAL.* This is the only right way to create a balance with both the Fire & Water within us all. Learn and educate yourselves and one-another by using the lessons provided by this planet of ours and Mother-Nature herself. Or do nothing and keep on going on spreading pain and suffering over minor misunderstandings and conflicts. AGAIN the choices are yours to take. No Insurance company or Political leader will carry such burdens without becoming corrupted themselves somehow. You cannot expect them to do what you are not willing to!

(**The Security & Arms Race**)

You all have probably already noticed <u>Governments and their security and defense representatives, are asking for bigger budgets</u>. Of-course they are! Have you ever encountered any governmental department stating it could do with less the following year? Of-course you didn't.

Every time any government makes something illegal or starts a war on anything, this only seems to enlarge the problem. The WarOnDrugs, only created a Global growing problem with these same drugs. The WarOnTerror did the same. Only giving way to many extremist minorities to gain ground.

Not only Islamic extremists, but also the Nationalists and all other groups who want to exploit their minority status became TV headlines following 9/11 and the subsequent WarOnTerror.

When the US forbid the word ,'fuck', one TV replacing it with bleeps, it became the most used word around the World?!Even our war against bacteria with Antibiotics resulted in Antibiotic resistant strains, instead of flew resistant people?!

Every time some ,'narrow minded', grey suite thinks to take away individual responsibility and liability, by creating some stupid law.

It gives way to it's citizens to challenge this law or leave it's application completely in the hands of the ruling authority. Thereby again only giving way to abuse and eroding morality.

Especially with arms & security and the Military Industrial Complex lead us to other side effects which I call,'feeding the Devil'. Whenever people are working in the arms and/or security sector they will start to become preoccupied with their tasks in a form of occupational deformation. Forced by the way the hierarchy is put together, these people will start to see problems where they do not exist. In some cases they will even resort to creating problems to get their annual budgets or sell their need for new toys (weapons) and get more staff.

Recently we have seen an unprecedented worldwide arms race taking place again, where all countries are spending increasing and staggering amounts of money on ,'so called', security & defence. What they forget to mention is the fact that most wars around the World are being fought with western arms and weapons in the first place. These are mostly bought by corrupt government officials in developing nations, paid by in Oil, Gold, Timber or other mineral wealth these countries have. Thereby rendering these countries again helpless and further away of ever reaching rising living standards. The multinational corporations are working with the same methods as a dealer or pusher would do, selling to his junkie clientèle.

The modern arms Industry was created to support Democracy & Freedom and form a deterrence against Dictators and other mindsets that would lead the World into chaos. These days they themselves have become the bringers of Chaos just by looking for profits.

The biggest danger of these methods are becoming more & more apparent in our modern digital world. The information world is quickly becoming smaller and technical developments are increasing ever faster. We could easily set about in changing the world and leaving the ways of the old behind us, if it were not for these old relics and their retarded mindset. We could create infra-structures in water, food, housing and sanitation for all people everywhere. Thereby creating work and growing economies for the next 100 years. We have the know-how and means.

Yet the ruling elite keeps on selling fearmongerin and the story that the world cannot sustain 7 or 9 billion people. So they rather keep on creating chaos and spread disease in order to decimate the global population, instead of marketing a unified vision for future development of our species.

This is why at present people are played against one another, in tribal, racial, religious or sexual wars. This is the way of the old colonialists.

This is the way of the narrow minded dinosaurs that are ruling our planet at present. The paedophile Nazi's ;like the Rothschild's and such. They still fight for dominance or just to stay in place. There is no unified vision that could be sold and marketed to the world, "like at one point Democracy sold itself in the middle of the 20st Century and is what made the Berlin wall fall and brought an end to the Cold-War between Russia and the US". Our leaders lack vision and are caught-up in their silly expensive summits that produce very little progress on any field. It seems to me that they are suffering from tunnel vision and consider themselves overly important. So they want to be protected against their own people, instead of really protecting their people. And there begins the warping of the brain and the job deformations. We need to protect these people against their own thoughts. Their preoccupation with security will create less freedom & privacy and more and more sophisticated weapons to be used at one point or another against one another. They will not deter from war and deplete all our human resources for all the wrong reasons. Our human history will stay filled with the ignorance of wars. Our planet will ,'at one point', shake its rear end just to get rid of the pests living on it and keep on turning, while we as a species will have accomplished close to nothing. Some elite will try to flee into space with some toys they made to no avail, and mankind will be reduced to the ashes of history.

The saddest part is the fact, that we actually are able to change and turn things around. We are capable of creating a brighter future for all. Yes we can! However our Political Leaders and the CEO's of the large multinational companies lack the willpower and decisive speed to do just that. They are stuck in their ways, slow afraid and greedy they are merely pretending to know what they are doing. They follow each other's example and fall in-line at every turn. And sitting behind their oak desks, in big offices and palaces they have become detached from the planet and the people. They are as frustrated as the next person and just want a good life for themselves as long as it all lasts. This is their narrow spectrum.

Just remember an ever increasing war machine will lead to more insecurity, more environmental pollution, more depletion of our mineral wealth and above all less protection of people in general.

We the people mostly need only basics to survive and be happy, the rest is just frustration, marketing and nonsense. Stop feeding the Devil with your fears and wasting our home Planet Earth for generations to come. It can be done. Most people do not want wars. However give a few poor suckers some guns and pretty soon a country is at war. This how we have been divided through the Centuries. This is what we need to overcome. Do not fall for false petty promises and beautiful words coming to you from toxic souls. Stop letting these mentally sick individuals sell their crap to your children or you.

Wise up! Become actual grown-ups and grow up. Educate one another and accept the small differences of opinions that exist between people. Or by God, Allah, Yahweh or whatever belief you look for as a false sense of security, we all will perish and deservedly so. I am no fatalist, nor am I religious. Yet I do believe in our spiritual existence, and that it is only a stepping stone towards our creator. It is Time we take that next step. The Time is Now!

We need to stop fighting each other and focus on surviving natural disasters. That on itself will be hard enough. The only enemy is our own human imagination or maybe the lack of it.

Free your mind so finally,...your ass can follow.

27/ Is America exporting chaos and violence around the World?

Fair question I would say.
America has been behaving more and more frustrated by the year.
And just like a cat driven into a corner it becomes frightened of it's own future and might jus strike out towards anybody and everything at some moment in time. Frustration creates extremists.   Think about it!
Pretty soon all it has left from its former Glory, will be its immense arms arsenal and arrogance. And with a society so mentally derailed, it will always find brothers in arms or any other from of extremism.

I belief this thought should be carrefully considered by other Big Nations worldwide.

At present <u>America's biggest export product seems to be violence.</u>
In Games, Movies and TV series, they all breed violence and frustration.
Reality shows that lack moral guidance.
Even the TV series as ,'storage wars – repo – judge this or that', they all make money out of others peoples suffering. They dehumanize and desensitize people in their empathy towards others.
They sell us the ,'fear', as well as the so called security. They sell both the problem and its so called solution.

We Glorify programs with lawyers, cops, criminals and soldiers as if they where ,'normal'. I happen to believe doctors, carpenters, plumbers, farmers and such are the normal ones. But hey what do I know.

Lawyers, Criminals, Cops, where there's shit there's flies,....
But who is what in a land of lies?

Just look at any former American foreign colony. They are all in complete disorder and chaos. Even worse than any former European colony.
Why is that, what do you think?

Divide and conquer?
Well they did divide and plundered and pillaged, and anything they left behind look more like scourged-earth than conquered.
They also made sure the political landscape could not return to a Democratic state anytime soon, before they left.
Admittedly we all have histories that should render us less proud, but these guys,......They are something else.
The only heroes they ever created were those seen in their Hollywood movies. The movies that mostly have so much production value and so little fantasy or creativity. As if History didn't teach us nothing they are all too often laced with Roman and Nazi like stylings.

And what has Hollywood contributed to any society anywhere anyhow.
Where are the long-term goals and visions, for us too pass along?

We spread wars, suffering and disease whilst talking about peace and harmony as some hippie grown idea that lacks grounding and common sense. It seems easier for us humans to subscribe to the filosophy of war than to that of peace.
We allow the most sick coke sniffing psychopaths in suits to steal the future, for no reason at all and without punishment.
We spread mental illness as wildfire and than ask, 'what happened'?
What happened,..... we happened!
We the people, that gave way to minorities of extremists while most of us just want a simple good life.
We sell and sold false ideas of lack and wanting to keep frustration alive, just to feed the mouths of the monsters called industry. Where more is never enough. Where profits rule over people.

So some of us even hope for the ,'End of Days', while the others just don't care either way and carry on stealing and killing ad random.
A big but fucking chain of fraud and corruption came over our world. And it hasn't gone yet! We have not yet woken up. So maybe we all need to suffer some more? Well, what do I know right?

I would love to see a New World Order come about that brings all you cowards and butt fuckers in-line. It is just a shame that we ,'at present lack', the people with the right sense of mind, to come to one Global healthy Government..
In general, our leaders are still as sick in the head as we are.
I do not have faith in religions either, because we have corrupted those as well. So lets see how we will do in these coming times of rapid changes?
Will we wise-up or keep on selling silly fairy tales to our kids, leaving them behind with nothing more than nightmares,
and mindless mind-numbing futures as mere workers and consumers, without any physical and intellectual stimulus to grow and evolve, well?
Choose and choose well you children of the Universe, because if there is a hell below,......... we will all,.... gonna .... go!
At least here on Earth we will.

28/ The Age of Extremism

So go outside and look around you.

What do you see when you look at the people?

Do you think that all want to be rich or famous?

I am here to tell you that, that is not the case.

No matter what industry and Hollywood try to sell and tell you!

Most people just want to live a normal healthy life.

Most people do not mind going to work and growing old, whilst enjoying lives little pleasures. For most people good, is good enough.

Now there are forces at work that would like us to believe otherwise.

These forces,' you know who ', want you all to live in a constant state of frustration. It helps them stay in power while we fight amongst ourselves over nothing and nonsense and buy their goods like good little consumers and wage-slaves. That is the simple truth!

According to them economy needs constant growth to sustain itself. This of course is nonsense. What the world needs now are stabilizing factors and real leaders, not all these narrow minded extremists that currently rule our financial climate. These days need to be over! Even if only for the simple reason that we as a species need to all get to the next level.

What we do not need is civil wars raining the planet for the next 100 years.

This however is exactly what will happen if ,' We the People', leave the future to our present financial and political elite. Right now through the present currency war, actual wars could arise. And I do not mean little ones like the Afghan or Iraq wars.

What should also be pretty clear by now is the fact that, 'extremism breeds extremists'.

Since the American one sided declaration of war on Muslim fundamentalism, radicals on all sides have popped up their ugly heads, left and right. Nowadays anybody and anything that does not suite a government, will be classified as terrorism. More and more we see governments take position against their own citizens, undermining Universal human rights as they go along. Democracies turning into federal ruled entities that fail the rights of the poor and protect those of fraudsters and economic values.

They are slowly turning all values inside-out and up-side down in order to maintain their elitist growing perversions. They are turning the entire world into a Sodom and Gomorrah.

These developments have nothing good in store for our sort. Remember our sort,... the Humans!

So like we can all read in our history books, minorities are still turned against each other. ,'They', still love to watch others fight and kill each other while they laugh all the way to the bank. Ruthless and without remorse, they keep setting up people against one another where and whenever they can. Nothing has changed over the ages!

The people haven't learned and the leaders haven't changed. We say we love our children and fuck-up their future daily. We spread disease and pollute in the name of progress and stupid gadgets.

Now,.. there is nothing wrong with science!

It is how we put it to use, ... isn't it?

Now why should we spend fortunes on arms and technological endeavors, when most in the world still have no running water, food or roofs over their head?

Why should dumb macho fucks in Africa, America or South America still have money for arms and bullets, but no money to feed their own fellow human beings. Are we still so stupid we fall for bribes of beads or plastic chains? The answer seems to be,.. ...   yes we are!

Why does the United nations have an offensive and defensive army, but no quick response unites for natural disasters? Answer me that.

Have we lost all sense of direction? Who will set us straight than?
Modern politics would rather support banks than people, so there!

Why don't we just arm everybody everywhere, and lets get it over with! Maybe that is the answer to our lack of effort?

Maybe more real pain and suffering will save us from our present, 'fuck it all', mentality?

However,.......... I still believe that most people can be happy with a simple life and a healthy life-style.

And now for the first time in the history of our species, we have the means to make this come about.

We just have to do away with these narrow-minded elitist minorities that are keeping this evolution from happening.   It is that simple.

The Oligarchs and Plutocrats, the Industrial and Financial elite should be held responsible for their actions, Now! This World, Our Planet has become too small for these hookers, Pimps and small time gamblers. They might have big cars, houses, tits and teeth, but their minds are as small as always. Now more than ever they are paranoid and more dangerous than ever before.

They have become dangerous to themselves and even their own loved ones, although they would rather die than admit this to be true.

Still most people in the world would not mind a Global government if it would assure their respective cultures and values. If it would give them a sense of a future a focus on the horizon for all, instead of this narrow-minded back and forth between silly people and so called leaders, that lack any solutions themselves. No longer would people be played like fools over borders and religions that did not exist in the first place.

A World Order, yes and why not? But with an International Court of Justice that supersedes all boundaries. Liability rules for all Companies, Industry and politicians world-wide Now!

That would finally put the fear of God in these perverts and   socio-paths that undermine our collective evolution.

Create a new cooperation between all secret services world-wide, as we know is already happening at present. For the people by the people, and I do not mean some stupid 2D films, but real life 3D action. Is this a call to arms, no it is not. It is a call to start using sense and real intelligence.

Arms as a last resort and they should not be pointed at each other but at the top, if needed.

Now maybe I could be called naive for having any faith left in us Humans. Time will tell. But, most people do not need much and the world and our survival will pose enough of a challenge to us all. We have to stop making it any harder that it needs to be.

We need to gradually level-out inequality and slowly start bringing the right infra-structures to all and everywhere. It can be done. All we need is the proper spoken words and actions by the proper role-models.

No more Politicians as Pop-stars and false Gods like actors and athletes. Real solutions for real life problems, Now!

Most of all we need to get the pressure of the pan and let-of some steam, so the Global situation can normalize.

This is what we owe to our children, so we'd better not wait too long. Agreed? Then spread the word and this article, translate it in any and all languages.

It is the least YOU can do! Make a beginning, be part of the re-start!

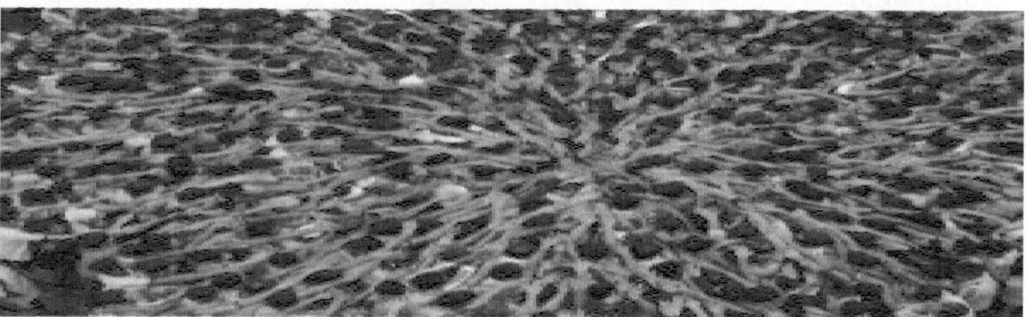

29/ How Society is purposely Polarized

....

It is obvious that people are purposely polarized by the ruling-elite. The ,'so called', minorities are being played by their respective leaders. The goal of this ludicrous game is to create diversion from actions of domination by this ruling elite and the creation of a new world order that has only a ruling-class & working-class. This means a total annihilation of any middle-class workers and citizens. The resulting civil tensions are believed to be useful to these filthy rich parasites of our Global hive. Already in the seventies they have made their calculations, that these rising tensions would probably only result in localized flares of ,'containable civil unrest', and so far this has come to be true. Even now we only see localized demonstrations that are met with strong and brutal police force. What is also plain as sight is the total disregard for any and all Human Rights by Governments and their Police minions. Power-for-a-few & National-interests & profits are obviously more important than people.

We the people, have obviously also not learned enough, not to be played-out against one another. We are fighting and killing each other for the littlest difference of opinions, thereby only creating more chaos and means for the ruling elite to dominate us. We the people fight over religions, sexual-preferences, tribal heritage, water, borders, flags and mere difference of opinions. But we are seemingly way too coward, ignorant and lazy to fight the bankers, financial-elite, insurance companies or other big corporations and governments. We seem to have laid down our senses and are no longer able to come together and fight for a better future for all. Through a lack of General-knowledge, we ventilate our frustrations on to our next of kin and neighbours as an easy way out for all our gathered bitterness. We the people are all loosing our collective connected fabric and falling apart like dust in the wind.

In an Ocean of radicalism, the Sound of Reason will easily be drowned!

This gives the ruling elite and sociopathic egocentric cocaine sniffing money sharks, the space to do with us as they please. And as we know from Machiavellian history, to divide is to rule. And we the stupid masses do not seem to learn from our passed Historical mistakes. Therefore we will continue to suffer and lose our progressive positive futures to a few sick minds. We will continue to chose bullets over rice and blood over harmony and progression. We will continue to be played in sick games of some detached and out-dated ideas.

Personally I am sure we could have already created a World with food and sanitation for all. We could have already created self-sufficient cities and communities. We could have already created free-energy transport systems.

However the false issues and distractions keep us from developing as we should. This and the Power brokers games, are holding us back from coming together in a true revolution of the mind.

Big-Oil, Big_Pharma, Chemical, Financial and other related Industries rule without hardly any control systems or legal restrictions. When they fail or fuck-up they are mostly not prosecuted as well as they should. When they contaminate entire ecological systems and turn nature into wasteland they sometimes pay a small fine and continue elsewhere. Our Food-Safety, general Health and Environment are at stake but who will pay the price? We are ruled by ignorant specialized thieves that only serve their shareholders interests.

There was no revolution when the bankers stole our pensions and taxes?!

There was no revolution of the collective when the Arab spring was turned into an Arab fall.

It's is just tribes and fractions fighting each other while the military-complex is cashing-in and is now creating drones to control us all from above like cowardly joy-stick warriors.

It's probably our lazy coward human nature that keeps us stupid and this combined with modern marketing techniques and scaremongering creates a World and Species in turmoil.

The New_Federal_Fascist_World_Order as is being experimented with in Europe and the US, could lead to a system that would make Hitler, Goebels and Mengele proud and that goes far beyond any past fascisms that we have ever witnessed in human history. But if we the People are not willing to make an effort in our minds and actions to change these proceedings as they occur, we might as well lay down our spirits & souls and any fight for civil-liberties and Human-rights now! We ,'the People', will than have been reduced to a footnote in Human History and we will have been finally been permanently been enslaved.The Revolution will not be televised, because it will not have occurred!

So choose and educate yourselves or shut up and suffer, these are your only choices. The process of dissemination has already been activated. The time to wise-up and act is now or never! Do away with false hierarchy's and it's monetary corrupt systems, educate yourselves or suffer the consequences.

Let's not forget that the true minority in this story of human-evolution, actually is the ruling-elite. And society will continue, with or without them!

So, ...The choice <u>really</u> is yours!

Because I am!

I have had enough of Political, Industrial or any so called Leaders, using ,'Us the People', as toys for their games and Wars.

It serves no purpose, no purpose at all. And all our leaders have done so far, is keeping our Planet divided and constantly on the brink of war or even World War 3. Political leaders just talk and hardly ever take real and actual responsibility for their decisions and actions in the creation of in- and external tensions. Industrial Leaders seem to only have eyes for the short term profit – growth and gains. These are the same people that by doing so, keep us humans here on this planet, from evolving to our next level in our common understanding and general awareness.

All the Industry at present that is being used for arms and weapons manufacturing, could be just as well used in the creation of renewable energy. clean water factories, infra-structure and distribution networks. This would mean work for millions of people worldwide, for decades to come. Or don't you think so? So lets blast the whole shabang to pieces again and start a new? Or live for decades to come in a constant state of multiple ongoing civil wars?

And the strangest thing to this attitude is the fact that the Big Companies already work in a World without borders. They ship money, goods and people all over the Planet on a daily basis. And they do this while,'we the people', are fighting ongoing battles over territory, religions, creed, color, or even sexual preferences?! So, that obviously means the World at present is only a free World for the Rich.

Now, where is the Democracy in that?

We want to conquer space, yet we are not even capable of taking care of this World? Now that is Pathetic!   And we call ourselves civilized, civilized from what? Civilized compared to monkeys, maybe?

What do we do to educate our young ones and properly develop their senses? Hardly enough, I would think. Proper Education is becoming even now more and more a ,'rich kid thing'. It seems to me we, ,'All the people', have not gotten the message passed on to us by our History. We either increase the World-wide suffering for our young ones and their off-spring, or we start to make a change to start again.

Its not like we could not wipe each other out several times over! The planet is stock-pill-ed to the brink with all kind off weapons. Nuclear, Chemical or otherwise.

So I guess with our present knowledge of technology, we have come at a turning point our existence where hard choices need to be made.

It is Time to turn our backs on the simple Machiavellian games of small time gamblers and corrupt officials. It is time to leave behind our present Kingdom's and hail in the coming of a new single Global Kingdom! The Kingdom of Planet Earth. A Blue shiny star in the heart of the Milky-Way Galaxy.

Our Blue Shiny Star!

I am ready for a Global Government, are you?

All these silly attempts for a United Europe or States, ... they lack a go getter mentality. They do not make sure we respect each others cultures and preserve our individual values. These endeavours are primarily based on economic principles, not human values! That, is why we should beyond our narrow-minded ways and think out of the box.

We know that Governments as well as Industry CEO's and secret services from all over the World, are meeting on a regular bases. From that point on we need to re-direct our armies and police into more humanitarian goals and endeavours. It is not as hard as it sounds and at the rate we messing up at the moment, pretty soon we will be forced to change,.......something somehow!

So my question to you All is,......?

Under the right circumstances and with the proper hierarchy, would you be willing to submit your and your loved ones future to a Global Government?

If so, just let us know and ,' like ', this article on Facebook. For now it won't cost you anything, it will just paint a picture of where we collectively stand in our growing mental evolution. And although we know it's not likely to happen tomorrow, it might just send out the proper message to those arrogant fellow fools in Davos.

31/ The contaminated Food-Chain

Welcome to the 21st Century boys and girls!

Welcome to the age of science and prosperity.

Welcome,......? I don't think so.

Our Industrial, Political and Financial leaders have proven themselves to be utterly incompetent. Our environment and subsequently our health have been radically compromised. Through an utter lack of responsibility and general awareness the Glorified Industrial-revolution could become our collective demise.

We have now soiled and contaminated both our our fresh Waterways, Oceans, Fields and Mountains. Residue of pesticides, growth and other hormones, antibiotics and anti-depressants as well as micro-plastics our now omnipresent in our complete food-chain. Face the facts.

What is wrong in our collective choices?

Why haven't we begun to rearrange our respective societies and called the master-of-Industry into question, or even jailed them? Our Global divide is with our present technological developments a direct threat to our collective well-being. Our narrow-minded vision of the future is leading us nowhere fast. We need to change our ways without further delay and start by creating an #International_court_of_law now. A court recognized by all Nations that has the right to pursue cross border infringements concerning human-rights and pollution. This court should be able to pursue all of those Financial, Industrial, and Political leaders that have misused their positions of power. The World and all humans have the right and obligation to themselves and their children to   get this done.

We simply cannot continue creating asbestos roof-plating in poorer countries or use depleted-Uranium armour-penetrating-shells in war-zones. Not to mention the fragmentation grenades left behind in Urban areas. We simply cannot continue creating random oil spills spraying those with even more toxic substances like Corexit and such. We simply cannot continue abusing that what was given, like ungrateful anti-social nitwits. We cannot sell the patents and licenses of life and mother nature herself to sick corporations like Monsanto. Even this planet has it's limits to what it can sustain and/or correct!

I do not care whether you believe in God, Allah, Jaw-eh, Buddha, in nothing or even Satan for that matter. I do not care whether you are male, female, lesbian, gay, trans-gender or alien. I do not give a flying shit who you think you are, or what group you hide behind, ...We need to wake up and smell the coffee. It is of our own collective making and is rapidly turning into one big poisonous soup.

Now we have developed some great ideas and systems that could save all our future enterprises. We have gathered some great new know-how that can quickly be put into play, so that real change can be established in a relative short space of time. It can be done! However,.. to get this ships bow properly lined-up, 'facing the right way ', we will first have to take the wind out of the sails of those that have no sense of sane human sentiments or those that are just cocaine   addicts and socio-paths.

This all has nothing to do with conspiracy-theories, religious or other nationalistic extremist fears. It is just something that needs to be done. It will not stand in the way of further technical developments in industry or internet and such. It will just *re-focus and re-adjust our goals.*

We just need to stop selling each-other those idiotic doomsday stories and get down to rebuilding our future from this point on. Fuck fame and fortune and all those that pursue it, they will be the real losers in this story, not you!

Get on the right side of history and start working on the creation of your children's future as it can be. Not these perverted images we have been imposing on them, but solid, sound, sane and full of real wonders of our own creation. Make yourselves proud and learned.

(& How Governments are hollowing out Constitutions.)

What is the Magna Carta? Basicly it is a 800 year old drafted form of a constitution, that prevents governments from taking authoritarian or autocratic rule over their constituents. It gives the ruling high courts the right to revoke or decline decisions made by governments or their houses of parliament. It served a real purpose for hundreds of years and has been updated as time went along.

At present several Governments including the Us and UK governments, are bypassing the high-courts more & more often under the pretext of terrorist threats as if their countries are in perpetual war with the World.

We have seen it after 9/11 when the so called ,'**Patriot Act**', threatened to undermine even further the remaining civil liberties in the United States. And we are witnessing it in 2015 when after the Paris **Charlie Hebdo** incident, many secret government agencies like MI5 the Dutch AIVD and the French Surté, were all asking for more funds and powers.

Simultaneously we are witnessing the right to legal representation for the average citizen becoming harder and harder to find in all so called Western Countries. This is Democracy being taking over by criminal corporate interests, as is forced upon us by treaties such as the TTP, TAFTA ,TTIP and whatever you want to call these contracts superseding governments and civil-liberties & Human-rights.

Is this what our ancestors have been fighting for?

So pretty soon we all will be interconnected through gadgets with our appliances at home or in the car, whilst eating polluted food, getting sick and than paying through the nose for medications that do not actually help either. That is how greedy corporations go; **Create the problem – Sell the solution**. It is not civilized. It can even be called dehumanizing. Down right dirty games by the filthy rich. If the majority does not rise up to stop this onslaught because of it's gradual inset, mankind is surely doomed. We need to educate each other on these matters, in order to find some future balance with ourselves and our surroundings.

Failing to do so will result in a more chaotic World wherein fake fear will be replaced by real fear and real hysteria. The filthy rich withdrawing behind closed fences while the world goes up in flames. Whoopdidoo. Try explaining that to your children. They will surely become even more fatalistic than you! Where is human intelligence in all of this? So much news-media so little sound information? So little proper education? To continue on the present road will lead to the collapse of our societies, and this collapse will affect all people everywhere rich and poor. Please show some intellect and avoid this from becoming a true prediction.

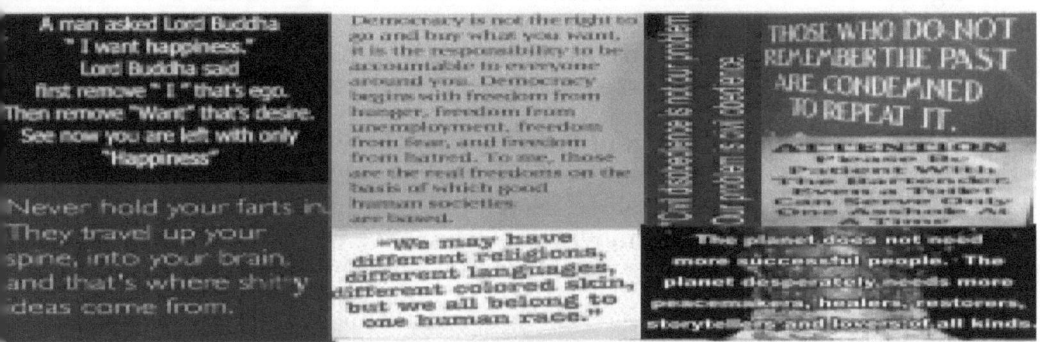

May 25th 2013 was not just any march or demonstration against some big corporation, this is a fight for the future of all Mankind. It was a global wake-up call to all humans with any shred of common-sense left in their hearts & minds. It is not just Monsanto that has lost all contact with all fellow human beings and the creator itself, many big corporations have lost track of what is right or wrong. What can and cannot be done.

Corporations such as Syngenta, Dupont, Dow Chemicals, Shell, BP, Unilever, Nestle and many, many others are putting profits before people.

Capitalism is failing like never before and are now posing a real danger to the future of us all. They as well as the modern pharmaceutical-industry, Bankers and Insurance companies have shown a real disconnect with humanity.

That is why I now call on the United Nations & the G8 for the creation of a International-Court of law that pursues any Company and their CEO's or Governmental representatives when they have implicated themselves in National or Cross-border crimes against humanity. These can be environmental as well the creation of health-hazards or consumer fraud. The World has become to small to let these white collar criminals continue their practices as before. The drive for money and profits are at present creating an environment that will create extremists because of growing corruption as well as growing inequality World-wide.

The right wing liberals in Politics have become extremists and even the parties on the left of the spectrum are not far behind in this general disconnect with the voters and the general public.

It seems Politicians have become career politicians instead of civil servants and are not able to withstand the pressure by corporate lobbyists. The results of their failing moral judgements are becoming more obvious by the day and can potentially lead to the collapse all Democratic systems.

We The People, need to address the growing concerns regarding fossil-fuel usage, Plastics pollution, Pesticides usage in large scale Mono-culture farming, the Genetic manipulation and engineering of nature and all such topics that are at present seemingly not well regulated and minimally monitored. It is what we owe to ourselves and our children, it is only normal or at least should be considered normal.

If the Gray suits of Industry and Politics lack the vision or competence to deal with these important issues, than they need to be overthrown and sidelined as soon as possible, so we can continue to work on the betterment of all societies anywhere! Otherwise we wont be able to pay the bill when Mother Earth presents it to us and her judgment could final!

Are ,'We the people', becoming aware of these modern self proclaimed gods of industry. Over the ages we, the people have been dominated.

Dominated through wars, fear and weapons. Nowadays we are dominated through our energy usage and financial systems.

The next field of domination and conquest by these humanly detached individuals is the control of our food and water supplies.

What we need to do is to educate our brothers and sisters and spread growing awareness over this latest kind of arrogance by captains of industry. This latest form of fascism that is threatening Democracies everywhere.

These CEO's and directors to multinational companies have lost touch with reality and some have even become mentally perverted. Their ideas and visions of our common future are deceitful and dangerous to us all.

Our Politicians need to step up and protect their citizens and consumers or be voted out in future elections.

What people do not need is left or right-wing extremism. We do not need any religious divisive extremism. What we need now is the sanity from us common folks.

We the silent majority need to speak up and show all extremists how wrong they are. We need to take the power back form these cocaine based psychopathic arrogant individuals which have clearly lost their way.

Our Future lies in Biodiversity not just mono-cultures and pesticides.

Let the seed exchange go from hand to hand around the Globe. Lets see which governmental lackey will put you in jail for sharing seeds? Which lackey or judge and slave to the industry will allow the patents of life and Mother Nature to become the property of just a few?

So spread your knowledge and teach your fellow human beings about this new creeping form of fascism.

In over 366 cities worldwide should be the start of a new and peaceful fight for Democracy. A new long and persistent peaceful fight for a World in growing harmony.

No patents on Life!   No laws on Seeds!

No new slow creeping fascism in Industry and Media!

What we do need is an International court of law that restores our faith in Politics and sends corporate or governmental criminals to jail.

No matter how rich or powerful they are!

This march is not about politics, it is about Universal Human Rights. It is about a basic quality of life for everyone. So do what you can do and spread this message of sanity around the Globe. Let these corporate kleptocratic corrupt individuals know that it is enough. Let them stop chipping away on our civil liberties. It's enough! Wise-up! It's enough!

"STRANGE TIMES ARE THESE IN WHICH WE LIVE WHEN OLD AND YOUNG ARE TAUGHT FALSEHOODS IN SCHOOL. AND THE PERSON THAT DARES TO TELL THE TRUTH IS CALLED AT ONCE A LUNATIC AND FOOL."

— PLATO (427 BC)

Watch a video report from the Amsterdam #MAM

33/ Wealth and Responsibility

Easier said than done!
We have become more and more focused on the gathering of wealth than
ever in human History before. This of course driven by marketing and
sales techniques of the larger Industrial cooperation's. We do not at all
think about the implications of our actions towards other fellow human
beings as long as we,'   have or get '.
As a species and as societies we have become totally anti-social and
radical extremists. Where does all the gold for your jewels or your
telephone gadgets come from? You don't care, now do you? As long as
you can play prince and princesses right? I know I am right.

It is more than obvious than ever, that the Industrial revolution, 'once
hailed as the new messiah', could become our   collective downfall.
We cannot have this new found wealth and build on it, without some
more sense growing along with it. We need to grow-up soon, or we will
perish all together because of some stupid slip-up by science or industry
and we need to do this rather sooner than later.

We need an emotional revolution! The growing inequality will breed
more extremism worldwide, it is only logic! The paranoia of governments
will breed anarchy, it only logic!
The human disconnect between population groups will breed wars and
chaos.
The dehumanization of people will create monsters of our own making.
IT IS ONLY LOGIC!

We need fair-play and fair-trade to become of age and prosper.
But how we do this is a totally different kind of problem, mainly because
of the many perverted forces that are at play at present
Those that have do not want to give, and those that do not have are willing
to take. The aggressiveness is growing out of proportion.
As children that lack oversight and emotional control we fight over toys
and dominance. Those that are supposed to be, 'grown-up' , sure as hell
don't show it!

So far we have perverted Industry, Sex, the environment and nature's
beauty itself! The media gives more air-time to criminals, frauds and
useless actors and popstars, than they do do those that do good. We seek
sensation and feed frustration. Now, that can hardly be called ,'healthy',
and while science seeks for answers on other planets to physical
questions, we increase the mess on our own planet beyond the point of no
return, daily. This way giving meaning to the phrase, Go fuck yourselves'!
This would also explain the increase of straight and gay bud-sex globally.
You sick perverted sociopathic monkeys, you!

And what is the result from our behaviour, so far?
We cannot trust our leaders, our bankers, our insurance companies, our
wives or husbands our, ... should I continue?

Damn I'm not proud people!
If this is the best we can do as a species, the Lord can bring on the floods as far as I am concerned. We will need a lot of water to wash away the many sins we perpetuated.

My mother once said to me that; people are not created bad or mean, but that they become that way!? Not any longer, I believe this.
I think mankind is a selfish and practical based chemical creature that does not understand its own functioning as much as it should.
When we say we love our children it is also a lie. We don't know what love is!

We believe whatever we are told. As Industrial marketing engineers know all too well. We are as clay in their hands and they mould us into brainless consumers and work-units. Packed closely together in urban surroundings we are fed with as little knowledge as possible and we are kept away from using our own minds to the fullest. Get up, stand up? I think not! ^>

We will silently undergo any treatment and social experiment until all our smiles and love have become but empty gestures and we become numb!
And that is where the Wealth and Responsibility should come into play!

In the meantime, we seem to wait for our saviour or messiah to come!
As if it is not our own responsibility to do good!
So to conclude this little get together,...... we don't know shit!
We pretend and claim the knowledge of ages and what we show as a result is a collective chain of fraudulence and corrupt butt-fuckers.
Now go and tell your children the truth if you dare, tell them,..

WE FUCKED UP!
We sold your future for a few trinkets to the fascist-Industrialists.

Tell your children that!
And now go and vote like it means something.

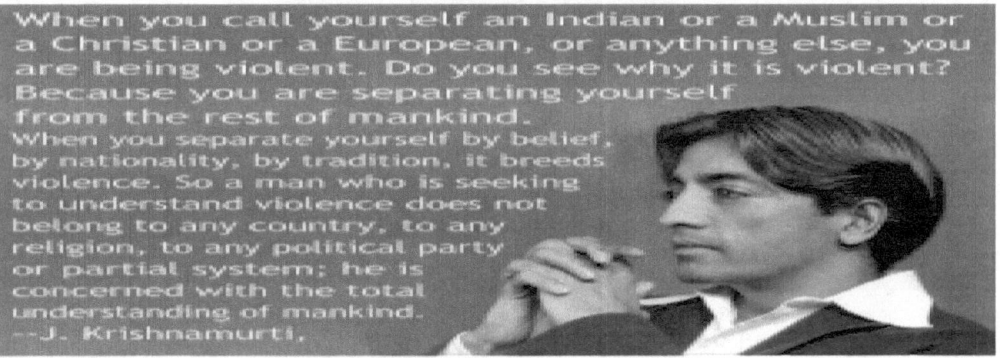

When you call yourself an Indian or a Muslim or a Christian or a European, or anything else, you are being violent. Do you see why it is violent? Because you are separating yourself from the rest of mankind. When you separate yourself by belief, by nationality, by tradition, it breeds violence. So a man who is seeking to understand violence does not belong to any country, to any religion, to any political party or partial system; he is concerned with the total understanding of mankind.
--J. Krishnamurti,

34/ Soul and Happiness in a modern society

One would hardly notice it in our modern day busy societies, but all too often we leave our Souls wanting. So occupied with outer appearances and the gathering of material wealth, we tend to forget our human sides. We are so occupied with our careers, looks, physique, games and gadgets and such that we do not notice how we are frustrating our souls. It is this individual behaviour that all too often results in a collective unhealthy mentality.

We have too experience everything once and all that we can and it all has to happen in this lifetime.
To just be working on spiritual growth and education, almost does not seem enough any more?
To be satisfied with the simple good things in life and peace of mind, would make us grow old gracefully and create wrinkles of happiness instead of wrinkles of worries. And why not?
Why are we letting ourselves be forced into continues frustration and unhappiness by the pushers of the marketing industry? For what? To get rich or try dying? By any means possible?
Regardless of others?

It is this predominant mentality that at present is eroding the fabric of our societies and humanity.
It is this what keeps our species from a steady evolutionary process.
It is this what holds us all back from progress in our social and emotional evolution.
It is being done to us and by us and not only socially and emotionally but simultaneously in technical fields as energy development, as well!

GETTING BACK TO THE REPLENISHMENT OF OUR SOULS.
Our souls need food too, just as do our body and brains.
What the soul needs however, is the oceans blue, mountains high, forests green, children smiling, arts and philosophy and such.
Shared acts of happiness and delight and the show of mutual appreciation.
It is good to sometimes be satisfied with what you've got, not frustrated with what you,'think', you lack!

Do not let TV tell you otherwise. Do not let these pushers of industry fool you into a frustrated sense of consumerism, where enough is never enough!
Where for every new millionaire thousands of people suffer or even perish and die!

Keep a watchful eye and mind out for this bunch of pedo-nazi's that at present seem to rule the world and mankind!
Their perverted message is ringing through in all we now create.

Especially so, it is clearly present in the media such as, movies, music and the gaming industry.
The last and former are heavily founded with money from the weapons-industry that in times of crisis can still make 500 billion dollar turnover.

It seems we cannot shake our ancient colonial mentality that has served us well so far, but is now in the way of progress and makes us keep on repeating the same mistakes.
The lessons of History either seem to lack impact or people are sadomasochists and like the pain and suffering? How else is our continuous lack-off-effort to be explained?

Life will always be a struggle for education and survival. We need to be able to fight and withstand and overcome. Even if its only for natural disasters on this our violent but beautiful planet.
So we do not have to make it harder than it is, but we do!
We take on shitloads of manipulation through regulation that only serve to undermine our individual sense of responsibility and general awareness.
In the meantime we are being picked-clean by predators like banks and insurance companies.
Our souls get caught in an ongoing tug of war between conflicting interests, lack of vision and general narrow-mindedness from ourselves and our ,'so called', leaders.
What we end-up with is just a bunch of emotional infantile monkeys playing with high-tech gadgets
And the money and gadgets are not the problem, we are!

We need to make the next step into a future that shines brighter for all!
We need to start creating soul-food again! Replenish our souls!
Start the next phase in our human social and emotional evolution.
The time is now to Thrive!

Do not talk about love. Talk is poison! Show your love!
Clean up your act and get a move on!
Your not alone, when your heart is your home, your never alone!
So don't listen to TV, listen to me,

Trinityroy,........your Urban Guru & Doctor of soul!

Life
is not Heaven or Hell
Black or White
Happy or Sad
Hetero or Gay
People and Life are not that simple
Neither is using your minds, so Start Already!